CUBA AND ME

CUBA AND ME
LOST IN THE EYE OF A HURRICANE

Sally Corbin Jacobson

TATE PUBLISHING
AND ENTERPRISES, LLC

Cuba and Me
Copyright © 2013 by Sally Corbin Jacobson. All rights reserved.

No part of this publication may be reproduced, stored in a retrieval system or transmitted in any way by any means, electronic, mechanical, photocopy, recording or otherwise without the prior permission of the author except as provided by USA copyright law.

The opinions expressed by the author are not necessarily those of Tate Publishing, LLC.

This book is designed to provide accurate and authoritative information with regard to the subject matter covered. This information is given with the understanding that neither the author nor Tate Publishing, LLC is engaged in rendering legal, professional advice. Since the details of your situation are fact dependent, you should additionally seek the services of a competent professional.

Published by Tate Publishing & Enterprises, LLC
127 E. Trade Center Terrace | Mustang, Oklahoma 73064 USA
1.888.361.9473 | www.tatepublishing.com

Tate Publishing is committed to excellence in the publishing industry. The company reflects the philosophy established by the founders, based on Psalm 68:11,
"The Lord gave the word and great was the company of those who published it."

Book design copyright © 2013 by Tate Publishing, LLC. All rights reserved.
Cover design by Samson Lim
Interior design by Joana Quilantang

Published in the United States of America

ISBN: 978-1-62510-356-7
1. Biography & Autobiography / General
2. Biography & Autobiography / Cultural Heritage
13.03.22

DEDICATION

To all of you who have asked, "Why were you in Cuba?" or "Was your father in the military?" or "So you can speak Spanish…really?"

To my sons Carl and Ricky. I hope you love reading this as much as I've enjoyed writing it. Over the years, you have read bits and pieces that I have written about my childhood in Cuba. You have urged me to get it all down. You wanted to know what my roots were and where your maternal ancestors came from. You didn't know your great grandparents or your grandmother, and only your grandfather for a short while. I bring them to you on these pages so you can know them a little more and love them as I do. I know they already love you. You have never been to Cuba, and it is hard to relate to. I hope this story brings it closer to you. Guys, this is a simple story. Everything I wrote about really happened.

And to all my friends and classmates who were there too and shared many of these experiences.

ACKNOWLEDGMENTS

Special thanks to my brother John Richard Corbin and my husband, Terry Jacobson. Your patience, input, editing, and support gave me the courage to finally (after fifty years) gather the memories, past writings, ancient photos, and details into this story before it loses its "muchness." (Mr. Nuendorf, my sophomore teacher at Ruston Academy, said that *muchness* was a "nice word" when I once used it in a composition I wrote).

CONTENTS

Prologue --- 11

Part 1: The Journey: Are We There Yet? ------------ 19
    Home Again ------------------------------- 21
    New Year's Day, 1959 (Havana, Cuba) ----- 24
    La Familia (The Family) ------------------ 27
    Paradise Lost ----------------------------- 33
    Paradise Found --------------------------- 37
    Storm Brewing --------------------------- 61
    Eye of the Hurricane --------------------- 73

Part 2: Hello, USA ----------------------------------- 87
    The Aftermath --------------------------- 89
    Hello, USA ------------------------------- 89
    Whistles and Gunshots ------------------- 93
    Reconnecting ---------------------------- 95

Part 3: How Did We Get There? --------------------99
    The Anglo-Hispanic Frontier --------------101
    Americans in Cuba -----------------------109
    Americans of Cuba -----------------------117

References and Acknowledgments ----------------125

PROLOGUE

"I Could Hear the Telephone Ringing"

By John Corbin

I could hear the telephone ringing in the house as I came up the drive. It was about six o'clock in the morning on the first day of 1959. I was eighteen years old, back home in Havana for the Christmas break after my first term at the University of Chicago, pleased to have spent New Year's Eve at parties with my schoolmates from Ruston Academy, the American school in Havana from which I had graduated the previous spring.

The telephone call was for me. It was Sol Henriquez, a girl I had been seeing. She was excited. "I had to call you!

Batista has fallen! He's fled the country! The revolution has triumphed!"

For the next few days, Havana closed down. The police were nowhere to be seen, businesses and offices stayed shut, flights were cancelled, and busses weren't running. Most people stayed home, waiting for news from the radio and television, which at first broadcasted little more than recorded calls for calm and prudence. Only the politically active were in the streets, taking over government agencies and breaking into the homes of members of the Batista regime, most of whom had also fled.

I spent these days on my own "guarding" Delmonico, the family restaurant, which was fortunately only a few minutes' walk from our house. I was given this task because I was the only male in my family who sounded Cuban when speaking Spanish. The women, my sister and my mother, who, like me, had been born and raised in Cuba, and my grandmother, who had come to Cuba at the age of eleven, all spoke Spanish without a trace of foreign accent, but standing guard was not thought appropriate for women. The other men of the family, my father and grandfather, had come to Cuba as young American men, and though they now spoke fluent Spanish, their accents were still unmistakably American. So I was thought the least likely to provoke anti-American feeling in Cuban revolutionaries, should any appear. In the end, there was little to break the silence, and no threat at all to the restaurant from revolutionaries. Early on, a very small man on a motorcycle with a very big man in the sidecar holding a rifle drove up and parked. They said they had decided to mount a patrol to maintain order. I explained that the restaurant was closed but there had been no disturbance. They asked whether I could serve them Cokes. I did, and when they finished, each handed me five cents. Accustomed to the previous regime where the police who stopped by for hamburgers and Cokes were never charged, I refused. They insisted, saying that now with the revolution, everything would be different. I thought it best to accept, but didn't have the heart to tell them that the normal price was ten cents.

The next day, Roger, one of the waiters, came by with several men. He announced that they had come from taking over the Instituto del Cafe, pulling a revolver from his belt and waving it excitedly, but not threateningly, as he talked. Later he became a militant pushing to take over the restaurant in the name of the revolution.

Later still, Sol dropped by with her father. They had been working as volunteers for the Cuban Red Cross and were full of enthusiasm and admiration for the doctors and nurses working for the revolution.

People were waiting to see what would happen, and the focus was on Fidel Castro, leader of the main armed revolutionary forces in the mountains of eastern Cuba. When he came down from the Sierra Maestra and started moving west, it became clear that his was to be a slow triumphal procession for he stopped frequently to give speeches, and his speeches were eloquent, entrancing, and very, very long. In Havana, we were still waiting.

As the streets were now safe, I dropped by Ruston to see Boris Goldenberg, one of my old teachers, who lived in bachelor quarters in the school. Boris had a PhD in history from the University of Heidelberg, where he had joined the student Communists. Jewish as well as Communist, he had to leave Germany when the Nazis came to power. He settled in Paris and once again had to flee when the Germans invaded. The United States refused him a visa because of his Communist affiliation. Cuba was one of the few that offered a visa, and he gratefully accepted it. At first he worked as an advisor to various political parties; later he became a teacher of modern European history at Ruston. So the Communist refused entry to the United States found himself teaching the sons and daughters of American diplomats and big company executives in an American high school in Cuba. His lectures on the Bolshevik Revolution were legendary, lasting for weeks and heard all over the school.

Boris had been keenly watching developments since Batista had fallen and had particularly monitored Castro's triumphal procession, still only halfway to Havana. "I have now listened to thirteen hours of Castro's speeches, and I can tell you one thing. Whatever else he may be, he is not a *caballero Catolico*, for not once in those thirteen hours has he mentioned the word *God*."

This was a reference to an argument that Castro could not be a Communist because he had been educated by Jesuits and was therefore a "Catholic gentleman." When the Communists did come to power in revolutionary Cuba, Boris was forced to leave again for he was a Trotskyite. He would, however, write the first major history in English of the Cuban Revolution and its consequences for Latin America, a book much informed by his direct observations and personal experiences.

My father, with a long experience of politics in Cuba, dismissed the revolution as yet another episode of the outs wanting to get in, but I was not so sure. When, after about a week, we received word that a special flight had been organized to get American college students back to the United States so they could resume their studies, I refused to go. I wanted to stay, at least until Castro got to Havana.

He finally arrived nine days after Batista fell. Sol invited me to join her family, who in turn had been invited by friends who lived in an apartment on the Malecon, the seafront road up which Castro was scheduled to travel, to watch his arrival from the top of their building. As we made our way through the excited crowd to repeated shouts of "Viva la Revolucion!", "Viva los barbudos!" (bearded ones), and even one of "Viva los patilludos!" (sideburned ones), the atmosphere was carnivalesque. The noise was only slightly muted when we got to the roof of the apartment building. From four stories up, we could see to our right the empty road lined by expectant people all the way to where it began at the entrance to the bay of Havana. As Castro was coming from the east, that was where the procession would first be seen. The first vehicle to turn into the Malecon was a battered jeep carrying about six armed and bearded men dressed in fatigues. Moving at walking speed, it was followed by similarly dressed men on foot and riding an assortment of jeeps, cars, trucks, and even a tank. All were cheered and applauded by the crowd as they passed. Finally Castro came into view, but it was impossible to tell what vehicle he was riding on or how many were riding it with him for as soon as he reached them, the people on both sidewalks surged into the street so that all that could be seen was a mass of humanity with a slight hump in the middle made up by those riding the vehicle. We watched this moving convergence of the Cuban populace as it approached, passed beneath us, and moved on west in the direction of Camp Columbia, the main military base of Havana that had been a primary source of Batista's power and was now, appropriately, the final destination of Castro's triumphal procession.

The next day I left for the United States. The only flight I could find was with the small local airline, Aerovias Q, which had just reinstated its service to Key West. From there I caught a Greyhound bus to Miami. A few miles outside of Key West, the bus was stopped by the state police. The trooper who mounted the bus announced as he moved down the aisle that he wanted each passenger in turn to state their name and place of birth. It seemed likely that he was looking for illegal immigrants from Cuba. Would I be detained if I said that my place of birth was Havana? Should I lie? In the end, I told the truth. He hesitated, scanned me again, thought for a second, and moved on. To him how I looked and sounded seemed to count for more than where I had been born.

I didn't know it then, but the revolution would end our home in Havana. I wouldn't be going back.

PART 1

The Journey: Are We There Yet?

HOME AGAIN

Pigtails and World War II, shoe buckles and Fidel Castro, grasshoppers on glaciers, whistling and gunshots…What do all these have to do with each other? They all connect into the story of my life. It's been one whirlwind of a journey.

Right now it's Christmas 2008, and I'm decorating my Christmas tree. I'm having trouble hanging my blue and red ornaments. They don't seem to match the magic of the red cardinals and blue jays on the snowy pines outside my window. The scene is breathtaking. The rolling snowy hills of Southwest Wisconsin form a beautiful canvas framed by my window.

It's my first Christmas in my new home. I am done with the labor pains of designing and building it into being. I need to celebrate its birth. I want every nook and cranny to sparkle with the holiday.

My husband Terry and I had moved from Chicago and became realtors when we found this property thirteen years ago. Our market was city people like us who wanted to build a home in the country, preferably by water. We were always on the lookout for accessible land with lakes or rivers. This was getting harder to find. We understood the need for quiet, mesmerizing space. When we stumbled on these twelve hilly acres, we knew we had found a gem. At the For Sale sign, we started walking down the long drive toward a wooded area. Seeing water shimmering behind the leaves, we broke into a run. Tearing through the last cover of branches was like unveiling the *Mona Lisa*. The crescent-shaped lake smiled at us and instantly owned us hook, line, and sinker. The paperwork was just a necessary formality.

Too excited to wait until we could build a new home, let alone dig a well and septic tank, we abandoned all reason along with our home in suburban Chicago and moved to Wisconsin. Dragging in an old blue mobile home, which we named Orca, we set up camp. So what if we didn't have plumbing? We had an outhouse and the lake. Our four dogs and cat were not as thrilled. Horrified, the dogs made a beeline back down the road. The cat found refuge under the floorboards of the bedroom, crawled the seventy-two-foot length of the trailer, and surfaced in the kitchen, quite disgusted over the journey.

The next day, we chopped branches and climbed trees that surrounded the lake, trying to determine the best view for our house. Knowing we would build soon, Terry's way of denying that we were now trailer dwellers was to refuse to even put up a towel rack. A year and a half later (I had the towel rack and plumbing by then), the house was finished. We decided to market the home to vacationers for a little while. It took off, so we decided to build more homes and rent them to vacationers, all the while patiently putting up with an aging, sagging trailer.

Each home was carefully designed to complement and fit into the surroundings. Over the next ten years, we added the things that arose out of our own needs to escape to nature: the hiking trail through the woods, the waterfall for the sound, the deck on the water to fish from, the trampoline on the water to swim to. And so "Birch Lake Secluded Getaway" grew and came into being.

Finally, we moved into the fifth and last house, taking our towel rack with us. It had been a long journey. The aging dogs and twenty-year-old cat were greatly relieved. Finally we were complete. Finally we were home. Now it's our first Christmas in our new home. We all snuggle on the leather couch, enjoying the warmth of the crackling fireplace. It's the perfect scenario for storytelling. I wish my mom were here to bring out a Charles Dickens book and read to us. I was feeling the need for the grounding traditions of the past, like ancient tribal fire dances or the hanging of Christmas stockings.

They anchor you to a past. Otherwise, it is like walking down a long street that is rolling up behind you as you walk. The longer the journey, the harder it is to see where you've come from. In my case, where I came from, the path totally disappears. I was born and raised in Havana, Cuba, of American parents, so while part of me is home, another part of me feels lost in the Atlantic in the middle of an impenetrable storm. As I look into the fire in my hearth in Wisconsin, I remember my mom's words reading "the burning logs give out the glow of many suns of long ago." And just like that, the path unrolls to long ago and to much warmer suns.

New Year's Day, 1959 (Havana, Cuba)

Christmas had been warm and sunny, as they always were on Christmases in Cuba for as far back as I could remember. We could never put up our tree before Christmas Eve because the tree would get too dry, and the needles would start to fall off. We wanted the tree to stay up until January 6, which was Kings Day. Our Cuban friends and godparents didn't give out presents until the three wise men showed up at the manger. It wasn't a very good Christmas for anyone that year. The political unrest of the Batista regime was coming to a climax. Tension was palpable in the dark streets, in the sparse theater audiences, and in the darkened houses where families hunkered anxiously around the radio as if awaiting news of an impending hurricane. Except hurricanes were familiar. We would wait it out behind boarded-up windows and doors as the wind threatened to beat us down. When the first wind died and the calm came, we knew it was not over. We were in the eye of the hurricane, a momentary lull in the middle of nowhere. In spite of the deceptive calm, we were in the center of chaos. There was no way out except to endure the rest of the hurricane. Then like the newly flattened grass, the inhabitants would spring back up as soon as the promised sun returns. Now, as we gathered around the radio on New Year's Day 1959, we were about to become a part of a new disaster. This one would not pass. This one would leave us uprooted and blindsided. We were about to be spit out of the eye of the hurricane. In those dark hours as I looked around at my family, memories came flooding back.

LA FAMILIA (THE FAMILY)

My first memory was the feeling of cold tile under my bare feet as I was released from confining arms. I ran across the room toward a mirror on the wall. My mother had been carrying me, and people were sitting around. I ran up to the mirror and made contact with the hands coming up to meet me. As I touched the hands, I realized with a shock that the image was me. "That's it? That's me? That's all?" was the feeling I had toward the tiny face staring back at me. Then I glanced at the images in the rest of the mirror and saw a familiar background. My brother Johnny was running toward me and took my hand. He was a little bigger than me, so I had to go with him. We tried to take off toward the back door and yard, but Granddaddy stopped us. Daddy picked me up high and took me to my grandmother Nona and Mommy, who were singing. I felt safe and happy. I belonged. I remember my first word in Spanish. We spoke

English at home except to our Spanish-speaking maid. I was making a big to-do about marching up the stairs. As I looked down at my feet stomping in front of me, I pointed at my Mary Jane patent-leather shoes and announced triumphantly, "*Zapato!*" Somehow I knew it was Spanish and not English. Somehow I already knew that my world was divided and yet one. We belonged here in Cuba. We weren't new. Granddaddy Fowler was born in Des Moines, Iowa. He came here as a young man to be one of the crew that was renovating Morro Castle.

Morro Castle, Havana Bay.

The Spaniards built El Morro in the early days of the colony at the entrance of Havana Bay to defend the city against other European powers and pirates. The walls had started to crumble.

Granddaddy was also an athlete and a boxer. He claimed to have known the famous boxer Gentleman Jim Corbett.

Granddaddy Fowler's rooftop gym.

When Granddaddy met and married Eunice Miller, my American-born grandmother who lived in Cuba, he opened up a gymnasium on the rooftop of the Havana city apartment where they lived. My grandmother (Nona, as my brother and I called her) was born in Ohio and moved to Cuba at the age of eleven, where she bonded easily with the Cuban people. Her two closest friends were two little Cuban girls. Estrella and Concha became her friends for life. Nona married my grandfather when she was fifteen. A year later she gave birth on the kitchen table to a stillborn whose umbilical cord was wrapped around its neck. Estrella was the midwife. A year later my mother, also named Eunice, was born.

Granddaddy, Mom, and Nona.

Estrella later had a son, Jorge, who became Johnny's godfather. Concha became Johnny's godmother. My godparents were also old-time Cuban friends. When my mother was seventeen, she met and married my father.

Enter John E. Corbin. Dad's family had lived in the Isle of Pines. *Isla de Pinos* was a tiny isle off the south coast of Cuba. Although Dad's father Sam had left Cuba and Dad was born in Chicago, Illinois, Dad came back to join his aunt Eva and sister Eleanor in Havana in 1930. He had graduated from college in Tampa. He became involved in many things, including publishing a magazine and running a radio show.

Eunice Fowler Corbin and John Corbin.

My paternal grandfather, Sam Corbin.

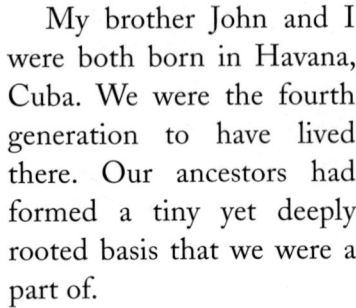

My brother John and I were both born in Havana, Cuba. We were the fourth generation to have lived there. Our ancestors had formed a tiny yet deeply rooted basis that we were a part of.

But then, things changed.

Us with Mom

Lil' Miss Zapatos

PARADISE LOST

When I was two and half, we left Cuba to go to South America. Granddaddy and Nona didn't come. The first place we lived in was Sao Paulo, Brazil. Johnny hurt himself, and his cries brought the town's children to our barred windows. Plastered against the rail, they laughed and pointed at the "*Americanos*." At night I was scared that some intruder was going to climb over the ten-foot cement patio wall with the broken glass chips sticking out of the top. I would lie frozen in my bed, sure that the shadows formed on the wall by the swaying palm outside my window would metamorphose and leap out at me the moment I closed my eyes. I couldn't get to my parents' room without first going out into the open patio. I was alone.

When I was four, we went to Rio. On the flight, one of the propellers stopped, and the plane made a sickening roller-coaster ride, landing at a small country airport. We sat for a long time on wooden benches that lined the walls, staring at the other passengers and at a group of men searching the grass in the field outside. When I asked my mother what they were looking for, she nonchalantly answered that they were looking for a missing plane part. When we left, we had to fly high, and it was so high everyone was sick, including some chickens that were on board. To this day I hate plane rides.

In Rio, we lived in the city in an apartment about four blocks from Copacabana Beach. We walked there every day to play in the miles of sand and ocean. We bought our little fox terrier from a beach vendor for four American dollars. When we got Spotty home, my mom spent a long time picking fleas off him and killing them in a bowl of kerosene. Johnny and I forgot Spanish to learn Portuguese. Our Brazilian maid would yell at Spotty "*Cachu du mato, perro du sato vais a la cocina!*" (Son of a cur, dog of a bitch, go to the kitchen!). Spotty hid with me under the bed covers.

One day Johnny cut my pigtails off playing barber. When my mother came home, she took one look at me, sat us down at the dining room table, and asked us what we had done.

"Nothing," we answered.

When she asked us again and we lied again, she said it was a bad thing to lie and that was why we had fought the Japanese. For a long time, Johnny and I felt very sad that we had started World War II.

When I was five, we left South America briefly and stayed in Miami for a year. That was where I experienced my first hurricane. We spent it in the grocery store next to our house. We sat with Alice and Cy, the owners, on orange crates in the aisle. A grocery store is a good place to hide from a hurricane. You can take your pick of food. We snuggled up in the dark while the wind howled outside and the trees doubled over. The only light came from the kerosene lamps. The only thing missing was Spotty. Mommy had left him at the house. After a long time, the wind stopped and the sun came out.

Mommy ran home to get Spotty. We were in the eye of the hurricane. Except for the broken branches and drenched grass, everything looked normal. When it started up again, I held a very grateful Spotty.

When I was six, we flew to Medellin, Colombia. We were going to live in a big house in the country. Before we landed, Daddy warned us how we would have to shake our shoes every morning to be sure no tarantulas had crawled into them. These big black hairy spiders had a vicious poisonous bite and could jump three feet. He also warned us about snakes. I had never seen a snake before.

The house was beautiful. Later in high school, when I was back in Cuba at Ruston Academy, in Mrs. Thurman's class I wrote:

> In Colombia we lived in a beautiful big two-story house on a winding dirt road. I remember clearly the big glass doors, huge terraces with decorated tile, and a large sloping front lawn with mango and orange trees. On the left side we had rows and clus-

ters of rosebushes, and along the right a small dirt road where barefooted boys and booted men herded cows and sheep to pasture. Standing on the lawn facing a mountain, I could pivot slowly, and my eyes could still see mountains towering over everything else, hemming me in."

Our house in Medellin, Colombia.

Spotty and I loved to run around in the large yard. He would bark at the lizards and scare them away. One night I woke up and saw a form lying on the floor by my bed. It was curled up and snakelike. I was frozen. Spotty jumped out from under the covers and attacked it. After he was done, it was a pretty chewed-up bathrobe sash.

PARADISE FOUND

When I was seven, we went back to Cuba. My grandparents were waiting with open arms. My dad was coming back to be a partner in Publicidad Inter-Americano, an advertising agency for American products sold in Cuba. When we got off the plane this time, I felt I was home. Mommy enrolled us right away in Cathedral School. I was going into second grade and Johnny into fourth. Before school even started, I had friends. I don't know how my parents knew the Harpers, but before we even got settled, Johnny and I were invited to a birthday party for one of the four Harper children. I would spend many happy sleepovers with Jeanie and her brothers, and we would create many imaginative adventures about our villain, "Mr. Gordon." It was an adventure we created that would be akin to Harry Potter today. Mrs. Harper would end up being my third grade teacher. She was one of those special teachers who stayed in your heart because she had the gift of loving what she did and loving her students for the individuals that we were. It was also her first class, so I lucked out on being a part of a group of students who would be even more special to her for that reason.

We eventually moved to my great aunt's country house thirty-five miles out of Havana. When she could no longer handle the forty-acre farm, we took over. My father took it on as a hobby. I took it on like a bee does a honeycomb. The land was soft and nurturing. The fruit tree branches bent with their offers of coconut, mango, avocados, mameys, guayabas, oranges, grapefruit, lime, and ciruela. Many of their limbs were wide enough to lie on. The sugarcane fields waved in the soft breeze. From the long dirt road, the towering royal palms led you into the driveway to the Spanish-style house that would be our home for the next three years. Past that, it circled around a huge mamey tree with a swing on it. At the end of the circle was a thatched-roof six-room *bohio* (a house with a palm leaf thatch roof over wooden walls and a hard-packed earthen floor). That was where our foreman, Julio, lived with his wife Fina, her father Manuel, and two daughters: Marta, who was my age, and her older sister, Margarita.

To this scene, add me, a tall, long-legged, blond, blue-eyed girl sitting in a mango tree, looking as out of place as a grasshopper on a glacier. Yet I was experiencing paradise. I answered my birthland in its own liquid tongue and danced to the beat of Latin living, however be it with a dash of fox-trot.

Long dirt road leading to the farm.

Julio's bohio.

Tropical paradise right on our farm.

Johnny let my pigtails grow, thus preventing World War III.

I remember waking to morning breezes floating through my screened window, bringing a rich scent of dew-bathed grass and newly plowed earth. I fling on a shirt and faded jeans cut off at the knees with Mom's pinking shears. The clean shiny tile is cool beneath my feet as I hurry to the breakfast room.

The breakfast room was always my favorite. The morning sun splashed through the vines that crawled up the barred window. Often a lizard warmed itself, plopped against the screen. In one corner of the room a huge old deep freeze was stocked with Nona's homemade pies and Daddy's homemade ice cream. Spread out on the orange-and-white-checked covered café table was a large chunk of doughy Cuban bread to be dipped into a cup of steaming milk with a dash of Cuban coffee. The *café con leche* was the only way I would drink milk. In South America, we had to drink reconstituted powdered milk, which had a chalky taste and would settle in chunks that I couldn't stomach. Although our farm milk was fresh and creamy, it was not homogenized and was still "chunky." I couldn't get past it. But I devoured the steamy *café con leche* and fresh fruit. Forget the boxed cereal that tasted like sweet metal.

Then Spotty and I would fly out the screen door, anxious to be out of the four-walled protection. First, we would stop by the work *bohio*. It was a small open thatched-roof area with a sink that Granddaddy took over for his projects. He made cottage cheese and fudge. It was also where the strawberries were brought in and boxed to be sold later in the city and town grocery stores. Sometimes he let me help. Small berries on the bottom, larger ones on top, the juiciest ones in my mouth.

Granddaddy also took care of the flower gardens and planted vegetables. He maintained his athletic interests by volunteering once a week on Thursday afternoons to the Mother's Club. The Mother's Club was formed by the women of the Anglo American community who wanted to provide organized activities for their children. Once a week after school, the kids that were involved would carpool from school to the Mothers Club. It was an important connection that enabled the kids from the different American schools to get to know each other. My brother and I attended elementary school at Cathedral School. There was also Ruston Academy, Lafayette, and St. Georges. Most of the kids who went there were like us, born in Cuba but with an American interest. There were many American business interests in Cuba at the time, such as Sears, Shell gas stations, Branif Airlines, and Sherwin-Williams to name a few.

The Mother's Club was one of the places we could all share our American selves. At the Mother's Club, we were a large strong community. Here, the mothers had the means to provide teenage tea parties, May Day celebrations involving dances celebrating the first of May, and a May Day Queen, who was elected by popular vote. We also enjoyed the large library, devouring the Bobbsey Twins, Joel Pepper, and the Hardy Boys series. But most of the activities revolved around organized sports. While most of the mothers sat and socialized on the clubhouse veranda, the kids enjoyed the track fields, ball fields, and basketball court. Granddaddy was one of the sports trainers/referees.

Granddaddy was always interested in health. He would come up behind me and straighten out my shoulders if I was slouching, turn up the light if I was reading, and tell me to chew my food well—even my milk! He would also try to "train" me in my athletic abilities. One of the routines was to take one of my grandmother's stockings and fill it with sand and tie it around my waist. Then he would have me sprint up and down our long driveway while he stood at the end with a stopwatch. Flying down the driveway as fast as I could, I would focus on him, and it helped pull me in to the finish line.

There is something very powerful to me still about that memory. It's a memory that still helps me "go for the finish" when I need to. When I'd cross the finish line, Granddaddy would read his watch and, looking pleased, he'd say softly, "You're an athlete."

On school days, Dad would drive Johnny and me to school. Cathedral School was in the suburb of Vedado, about an hour away. It was part of the Episcopal Church. All of the classes were taught in English, except for one hour a day of Spanish class. Every morning the classes would be marched across the grounds to the church for a half hour of services. One morning (I was in the fourth grade) during church services, I fell apart with an attack of the giggles. Oswaldo, the class clown, was making faces. When we were back in the classroom my teacher sought to reprimand me in front of the class.

"Do you understand that the church is the house of God?'

"Yes."

"As an Episcopalian laughing in your church, aren't you ashamed?'

"I'm not an Episcopalian."

"What are you? A Catholic?"

I thought for a second and went for the finish. "No, I'm an athlete."

The class got to laugh, and I got to stand in the corner until recess.

That evening, I searched out my grandmother for answers. I found her in the kitchen. Nona was in charge of the family meals, although Winnie, our Jamaican maid, helped her. Over the smell of chicken fricassee, I asked her, "Does God love me?"

"Yes."

"Why?"

"Because God is love, and so are you."

At the dinner table that night, we passed platters of chicken fricassee, saffron rice, and yucca with *mojo*, a garlic marinade. The conversation was lively. Johnny wanted Dad's opinion on a book he was reading. Mom and Nona discussed the costumes they had to wear in a little theater play they were in at the Community House. Granddaddy thought he should get larger cottage cheese containers. Dessert was my favorite: Winnie's Jamaican bread pudding. Full of raisins and rum sauce and lulled by family conversation, I sighed contentedly. Bliss was here. God was here too. He was all over the place.

After dinner was homework time. I hated homework. Mommy was in charge of this. Reading was not a problem. I loved to read. I had been reading on my own since I was five. We didn't have a TV. Mommy read to us. One day, right in the middle of *Curdie and the Princess*, she put the book down and announced that if I wanted to know what happened, I would have to read it myself. And so I did. Mom was a good teacher. It was the routine and discipline of school that I rebelled against. I felt stifled.

Then Saturday would come around again and liberate me. Spotty and I would run to Julio's *bohio* to get Marta. Then it was play all day with no restrictions. We seldom came back to the house until dinner.

Saturdays were usually the busiest, with my dad home to supervise any new project. We might witness the plowing of a field with a new modern tractor being operated by a reluctant Julio. His brown face oozed sweat easily under the floppy-brimmed straw hat, and his nervous cheek twitched, setting his mouth to making quick spitting noises as if to get rid of a speck of tobacco on his tongue. He cursed vividly at Miguel and Antonio, the two small hired boys from down the road. As they laughed and tried to climb up on the moving tractor, Julio squinted across the field and yelled at the white-clad figure who was picking his way slowly toward us. "Ay viejo! Apurate!" He would admonish the old man to hurry. He was impatient for the steaming little cup of strong, sweet, black coffee that Manuel was in charge of bringing. Julio blinked, sputtered, and muttered while the old father-in-law took forever to get there. Though it was his only duty, he wasn't about to break his neck over it for he was old, white bearded, and wrinkle skinned. He crept along, enjoying his journey and wailing a tuneless song that he made the words up as he went along.

My brother shot a crow with his new BB gun, and we buried it solemnly in a coffin with flowers and a headstone. Marta and I made the bouquet while Miguel and Antonio lowered the little coffin into the hole my brother had dug. After the ceremony, Marta and I left, for the boys made us feel happily uncomfortable. We did not belong with them. We were girls; their solemn, polite manner had been disciplined to this fact since they were born.

We sat in trees and picked fruit. By noon we had eaten our fill of oranges and mangoes and saturated ourselves with the metallic-tasting springwater from the ground faucets, taking care not to swallow any of the long thin green moss that would occasionally spurt out. Sometimes we soaked our feet in the cattle watering tank, letting the little tadpoles nibble at our toes until we couldn't stand the tickle. Or sometimes we watched the men unearth huge nests of *bibijagua*, an army ant with a vicious bite. These nests were four feet deep and six feet wide and, when uncovered, revealed a black mass moving among millions of white unhatched eggs.

At four o'clock, Marta and I would run to the cow pasture to watch the milking. Julio put out boxes of grain and called the cows, who were already on their way. All the children and men gathered here at this time. As a long row of warm, foamy, milk-filled pails were lined up in the grass, we all laughed and exchanged stories while the men milked and swatted at the flies.

Occasionally, a young worker from a neighboring farm came over. Marta was sure he was in love with her. "How do you know?' I asked, startled.

"I just know," she said knowingly.

And that was that. She tossed her long silky black hair off her shoulders, and her large black eyes sparkled as we walked home in the late afternoon. Although we were only ten, she was very well developed, and I was very envious.

We found Marta's sister, Margarita, now fifteen, busy at the backyard sink washing her face. "She's getting ready for town tonight," Marta teased. We watched Margarita pat coarse rock salt on her face and then let it dry. We did the same, and I danced around as I felt the sharp sting on my sunburn. After fifteen minuets, we washed it off with cold water, feeling fresh and glowing.

"You can get the same effect by using toothpaste, although salt is better," Fina, their mother, advised.

I firmly believed her. Though her hair was streaked with white, her skin was smooth as milk glass.

When the fireflies started to appear, Marta, in the excitement of the preparation for going into town, asked me if I wanted to go along. Fina topped it by inviting me for dinner, and I raced home to beg Mom's permission.

Scoured clean and wearing a dress, I sat down at Fina's wooden table. It steamed with platters of black beans and white rice, green fried bananas pounded flat with one blow of her fist, sliced tomatoes and green pepper, and sliced avocado sprinkled with lime juice and olive oil. We all ate like pigs. Even the water in the tin cups was delicious. The chickens wandered in and out and picked at our feet, cackling for favors.

Everyone was ready to go except for the old grandfather. Manuel would not go outdoors because the moon was full and, therefore, he believed, harmful to him. Julio looked funny with his hair slicked down, and Fina's face was strange with lipstick.

Marta wore her red-and-white checked dress. Margarita wore the dress she had made that week. It gathered at one hip and was very tight.

"Did you notice her earrings?" Marta scoffed. "She thinks she can awaken that Pedro Cortina."

The old yellow bus rattled on to the cobblestone streets of El Cano and began to trickle off its excess load that hung on to the sides of the bus and doors. As the bus became less lopsided, it came to a full stop, screeching on loose hinges and settling in the dust with a wheeze. Saturday night passengers wearing their going-to-town manners politely but excitedly pushed their way down the aisle. Marta embarrassed Margarita and put me in a fit of giggles by accidentally planting her foot on an elegant and flustered young man's immaculate white shoe.

Marta grabbed my arm, and we were about to take off when Fina reined us in, giving us our orders and warning that we were to chaperone Margarita. Fina then departed for her sisters' house, and Julio went to the corner bodega where beer was sold and tables were provided out on the sidewalk for the men to play dominoes. Marta and I followed Margarita's slow parade up and down El Cano's two main streets, which ran about two blocks long. She picked her way over the uneven stones of the narrow sidewalk, stopping to wave now and then or chat through a long latticed window. At certain houses, she would stick her head through the open door to peer into the living room, calling out the inhabitants' names. The houses were built attached to one another, and the large doorways bordered the sidewalk so that one stepped from the street right into the living room. Most of the houses had front porches, which was very important, for this was the gathering spot for the family after the day's work was done. It also was the children's playroom and the stage where the maiden ladies of the family could display themselves, all dolled up after their four o'clock baths.

Margarita finally chose which porchload of young ladies she wanted to join. Marta and I, having safely delivered her to friends and a few matrons, made a beeline for the town auditorium where they were showing a movie. We each had fifty cents. That left us each twenty-five cents to buy soft drinks and homemade candy from the little boy who went up and down the aisle.

Though the movie had already started, everyone talked and moved about. The movie was in French, which no one could understand, nor could we read fast enough the Spanish subtitles that flashed across the bottom of the screen. So except during the love or battle scenes or the ending where the hero was dragging the dead heroine by her long yellow hair across the desert, everyone exchanged candy and got reacquainted with one another. Everyone affectionately called Marta "Martica" and called me "Americanita" or little American. It was just easier for them than trying to pronounce my name "Salion" (Sally Ann). (By adding the suffixes *-ita* and *–ica*, it implied friendliness [e.g., birdie vs. bird].)

Back in school where the students were a mixture of Cuban, Cuban American, or American, I shortened my name to just Sally or Sah-lee. My class of thirty students had names such as *Lisa, Jeanette, Rocky, David, Aurelio, Miguel, Humberto, Roberto, Carlos, Luz Maria, Elena, Zeyda,* and *John* to name a few. The only ones who had any trouble with pronouncing the Spanish names were the Americans fresh from the United States who didn't speak any Spanish. They were the only "foreigners."

One day I was faced off in the hallway by two of the "foreigners."

"What do you live in out in the country, a hut?" asked the redhead.

"Did you live with niggers in South America?" a fat fellow asked.

"I live in a big white house, and I never saw a nigger in my life!" I shouted, and then nonchalantly added, "I'm going to have a peanut butter and jelly sandwich for lunch. What are you having?"

"Baloney," said the redhead.

"Tamales for me," said the fat boy.

That evening, I was reading out loud from one of my books to Winnie while she ironed. It was something I did often, and we both enjoyed it. In turn she would let me help her with the cooking when Nona wasn't around. Suddenly, for no apparent reason, I looked up and said, "Winnie, I hate niggers!"

A strange look came over her, as if her black face would turn white if it could have. Somehow the truth dawned on me. "Winnie," I said softly and full of awe, "are you a nigger?"

She pulled herself up straight and nodded with great dignity. I didn't know where to look or what to say. What had I done? Was she mad at me? That night when my mother held me good night, I pushed my face against her softness and shut out the world.

Winnie with friend Spotty under guanabana trees.

My mom fit in well with both Cubans and Americans. With her dark brown hair, green eyes, soft rounded figure, and perfect accent in both languages, she was a homogenous blend. She and her friends spoke "Spanglish."

"Put this in the *escaparacion*, meaning escaparate (a hutch).

"What's the *que pasa*?" meaning "What's happening?"

"Hey, *chica*, no me *digas* you are going to wear that *trapo*, eh?" One of her childhood friends was Rosa. Rosa was a full Cuban but spoke English. Rosa's husband was a wealthy businessman. I loved to go to their elegant house in the suburbs and play with her daughter. Little Rosa Maria had a playroom with toys to die for. Little play kitchens and furniture and dolls with full wardrobes. Her birthday parties were always very elaborate. For one of them, I had to wear spotless white shoes because all the other little girls did and a frilly dress with at least five crinoline slips under it to make the dress stick way out—something I didn't like because my legs looked more toothpicky that way.

Rosa decided to have one of Rosa Maria's birthday parties at our farm. We had beautiful yards and gardens all around the house area. She had merry-go-rounds brought in, and there were tables full of beautiful pastries and sandwiches for the *merienda*. She hired Mandrake, the popular magician. All the little girls were asked to wear red-and-white checked dresses with puffy sleeves.

There were about fifty little girls and their mothers about to descend on our front yard. Mom had made my dress, and I was very excited. I had asked her if Marta could come. "She already has a red-and-white checked dress," I pointed out.

The day before the party, I had gone over to Marta's *bohio* to show her my new dress. She got her dress out and was going to put it on. For some reason, I suggested she try mine on, and I would put hers on. I remember the shock I felt when we turned around in our ginghams to face the mirror. Her dress had always looked normal on her. On me it looked faded and old. My dress on her looked brighter then it had on me. I realized I had never seen her in new clothes. Why hadn't I noticed that before?

On the day of the party, everything felt normal again. Marta didn't look faded, and I looked like a bright frilly toothpick.

On Sundays we often had guests come in from the suburbs. We would sit on the stone benches in the yard while we visited. My grandparents' friends from their church were usually there, Mr. and Mrs. Tucker and Miguel and Rebecca Jimenez, who drove my grandparents home from church. Little Silvia Jimenez was so shy she would hide in the car until I would coax her out with peekaboo games. Little did I know at the time that the Jimenezes would be instrumental in aiding my grandparents escape from Cuba.

My grandmother often served her popular fresh strawberry shortcake and pineapple upside-down cake. But when my dad gave a pig roast, everyone came. I loved it except for the killing part. I didn't like that. When Julio pierced the pig's heart, you could hear the squeal all the way across the fields. The gutted pig would then be laid on the table in the work *bohio*. Dad would make slits in the meat and insert garlic cloves. This was followed by a *mojo* (marinade) that involved *narangja agrida* (sour orange) or a combo of limes and orange mixed with garlic and seasonings. The pig was then wrapped in fresh-cut banana leaves and allowed to marinade overnight. The next day it was lowered into a pit of coals in the ground. We couldn't wait to devour it. In order for me to be able to do so, I had to convince myself that I had never known this pig. I stopped going down to the pigpen. They were cute and smart. Some of them I had known since they were babies. I stopped watching the pretty fluffy white chickens too. I still watched the milking. Thank God we didn't kill cows. When I ran home for supper, I was glad that the beef on the table would be from a stranger.

Dad, the barbeque master.

I loved it best when we all convened out on the lawn to serenade the sunsets. My parents and Nona loved to sing and were active in the musicals put on at the community house. We would sing *Oklahoma!* or *Where's Charley?* But I preferred the older ballads best. "Tramp, tramp, tramp, the boys are marching" and

> K–K-K-Katy, beautiful Katy
> You're the only g-g-g-girl that I adore
> When the m-m-moon shines
> Over the mountain
> I'll be waiting at the k-k-k-kitchen door.

And my favorite was this:

> Red sails in the sunset
> Way out on the sea
> Oh carry my loved ones
> Home safely to me

These words later inspired me to write a poem about how I flew over the ocean with Jonathan Livingston Seagull and my life.:

> Where sea and sky met
> Was ablaze with a glory
> Of red sails and sunset.

I was a hopeless romantic. Sunsets would be one of my passions and joys for the rest of my life. I reveled in that climactic brief burst of indescribable colors, like the gold and red of glowing fire setting behind the ocean.

Suppertime was also a highlight of my day and worth running home to at top speed. But one day as I approached the kitchen door, I tripped over the shoe mud scrapper thing that was anchored in the dirt floor just before the cement patio. I struggled to my feet, glanced at my arm, and screeched when I saw that my right forearm was bent at a right angle as if it had another elbow. My family came flying out the kitchen door. Dad took one look and ran for the car. I was hysterical and ran to Mommy. "You'll be all right," she said. I stopped crying. "Your arm is broken. We have to take you to the hospital."

"Will they have to have to cut my arm off?"

"Oh, no no no. You'll be fine. They are going to fix it."

In her arms I slipped into a safe, comfortable place in my head, observing from a safe distance every detail—the concerned looks on my grandparents' faces, the shocked and sympathetic looks from Fina and Margarita as we passed them on the driveway, the long ride to Vedado to the Anglo-American hospital where Johnny and I had been born. It was near our Cathedral School. The hospital staff explained everything they were doing and kept telling me what a good girl I was being. Everyone was amazed at how calm I was. I didn't understand why I shouldn't be. Mommy had said I would be all right. And she knew I would be because Daddy was there too. In Mommy's arms I would always be safe. If we were lost and afloat in the ocean, I would be safe in Mommy's arms. But without Daddy, we would be lost and afloat forever. He was the ship that brought us all home to safety. Without Daddy, we would be unprotected. If two fireflies flew at me in the dark appearing like two glowing eyes, it would be Mommy who would reassure me, and I always believed her. But it would be Daddy who always had the power to simply turn on the light.

While I was in the recovery room, Anita Wright slipped into my room. Anita was my brother's classmate and lived in the neighborhood. She wanted to be a nurse and hung around the hospital a lot. At school, she was always the first one there if anyone got hurt on the playground. Anita would graduate as valedictorian from the eighth grade. She would later attend Duke University with Jeanie Harper. One day Jeanie's mother would call us to tell us that Jeanie had just called, hysterical because Anita and four other student nurses had been instantly killed when their automobile was crushed between two semis. But I didn't know that right now in the hospital, and her presence was comforting.

Tales of Tuckers, Piano Lessons, Zeyda, and Child Geniuses

My soon-to-be eleven-year-old brother Johnny was a genius. That was hard to live with. I'd like to think I was a genius. Just before my ninth birthday, my mom said, "I can't believe you are going to be nine."

I thought about this for a moment ant then said, "You mean I've only been here for nine years?"

My mom smiled and said, "You are very wise."

I would rather be a genius. But I'm not. Johnny is a genius. He would later graduate from Ruston High School with two scholarships, one to Harvard and one to the University of Chicago.

My classmate Zeyda Ruga was a genius too. But she doesn't pick on me. Zeyda plays the piano like a professional grown-up. She would sit beside her grandmother and watch her play.

One day her grandmother called Zeyda's mother and said, "Do you hear that? That's not me playing. That's Zeyda." Zeyda's grandmother had gotten up in the middle of playing, and Zeyda picked it up and continued. At the time, Zeyda was only three years old. She would graduate from the eighth grade and go on to Ruston with me, Rocky, and Jeanette. But she would only go for one year before her father would make her drop out so she could become a professional concert pianist. She would end up marrying a violinist and tour all over the United States.

I begged Mommy to let me take piano lessons. She hired the pianist at Nona's church. Johnny and I would take the bus from school to Mrs. Tucker's house where the pianist was also teaching Paul, Mrs. Tucker's son. I wasn't a genius at piano either, but then neither was Johnny.

When I was eleven, we left the farm to move to the Havana suburbs. For the last time after school, Johnny and I rode the city bus to the end of the line. It was right where the suburbs ended and the country began. We sat and waited on a low stone wall that fronted one of the private beach clubs. Finally, Julio came puttering up in the *pisa y corre*, the old station wagon that he had nicknamed Step and Run. For the last time, it drove us through the winding roads. Just before we got to Arroyo Arenas, you could smell the change in the air. I filled my lungs with the fresh oxygen.

When we got home, Spotty and I wandered the fields, trying to say good-bye. I felt like Little Orphan Annie. We were leaving in the morning. I did not run to the *bohio* to get Marta as I always did. I could feel her waiting for me, but I could not say good-bye. At the farthest end of our property, I lay under a towering mango tree. This was my "no one can find me" spot. I looked straight up the trunk, letting the pattern of sun-streaked leaves and brilliant bits of blue sky work its therapy on me. I felt a growing sense of caution. In the city, would there be a playmate within walking distance? Where would we play? What would we do? In the city, where does one go for freedom? Here, I could always find my tree.

As we left the next day, I still could not say good-bye to Marta. Maybe if I didn't say good-bye, she wouldn't go away too.

STORM BREWING

I was only twelve, but things were changing. The males of the species were starting to treat me differently. Not the boys in school. In the seventh grade they were still brats. I was still in Cathedral School. Johnny had graduated from the eighth grade and was in high school at Ruston Academy.

Every day I would leave school and walk down to Linea Street and catch the public bus. It was called the *guagua*. In order to stop the *guagua*, you stood on a corner, any corner, and stuck your arm out. When you got on, the conductor fought his way to you, and you paid him the eight-cent fare. When you wanted to get off, you either yelled "Esquina" or pulled the cord to stop at the next corner with screeching brakes.

The bus was always packed: uniformed schoolchildren, men in *guayaberas* (loose-fitting starched white-pleated shirts), and hippy women in tight skirts. There was a lot of chattering going on. The conversations were loud and meant to be overheard. It was customary for strangers to participate. Sometimes while the traffic was stalled, the bus driver would get out and get a snack from a sidewalk vendor. No one reprimanded him. The *guaguero* (bus driver) was the bully of the road and object of many jokes. Leaning far back in his seat, humming a tune, cap pushed back on his head, he sailed through many red lights. The police ignored him.

To this scene, add me, daydreaming in the aisle, my schoolbooks pressed against my hip, the tip of my shoe carelessly pushed against the tip of a shoe belonging to a man who is seated beside a woman he has his arm around. The woman is holding up a newspaper in front of them. Slowly, it dawned on me that he had been ardently wiggling his toe against mine. He got off the next corner, taking his toe with him but leaving his message. I shuffled my schoolbooks nervously to my other hip. Suddenly, I was aware of how crowded the bus was.

In Miramar, I get off at Thirty-Second Street. As I walked the few blocks home, a man tried to stop me. When I ignored him, he went around the block and met me at the corner. When I ignored him again, he ran around the block once more, and it became a joke. This time he was waiting with a silly bit of memorized romantic poetry. I had to smile a little, and now he strutted away, his pride restored.

Now that we were settled in the fashionable suburbs of Havana, my Mom's friend Rosa insisted that we join one of the private beach clubs. Rosa belonged to Miramar Yacht Club. That summer we joined too, and Mom began taking

Johnny and me every day so that we could join the organized swimming activities. Under the instructors' coaching, we learned the butterfly, backstroke, breaststroke, and crawl strokes. We didn't make any friends there. While Mom and Rosa sat with the other moms, Johnny and I put up with an attitude from the other kids. Not only were we newcomers, but we were also "Americanos." I had never experienced this before and wondered why being called "Americana" instead of Sally felt insulting. I was one, wasn't I?

I was delighted when I found out that my classmate from Cathedral was also a member. Jeanette Lamas and I joined forces and became best friends. She was also an American Cuban. Her mom was from the United States, and her father was Cuban. Jeanette was born in Cuba. We were glad when summer was over, and we entered the eighth grade. Johnny was now in his second year at Ruston High School.

That winter came a changing tone. Stories of torture. Distant gunfire. Schools being dismissed early. One such day I was sitting in the classroom when gunfire exploded on the street in front of the school. We were afraid to go out in the hallway. Finally, a teacher came around to explain. There had been a car chase with open gunfire. Walking home that afternoon, I dove into a ditch when a car that was going by backfired. Attempts were being made on Batista's life. Rebel forces grew. One day in the newspaper, there was a picture of a young rebel sprawled out on the ground. In true uncensored style, they spared no gruesome details. It was a close-up of the dead face of one of my brother's classmates from Cathedral School. He must have been around seventeen.

I started looking for answers, praying, and reading Genesis in the Bible for comfort, but God sounded angry. I sometimes got off the bus to walk into one of the big beautiful churches. They were always empty. I sought out Nona again. "Does God still love me?"

"Of course," she answered.

"I want to go to your church," I announced.

When I walked into Nona's church, there was no crucifix or bleeding Jesus. On the wall over the pulpit were the large letters spelling out God Is Love. *Period*, I added in my head. I was happy to join Mrs. Tucker's Sunday school class along with her son Paul and my friend Patsy Marels from the Mother's Club. Silvia would have been in one of the younger classes but was too shy and stayed with her parents in church.

The summer Jeanette and I were in the eighth grade, we started catching the bus and going to MYC by ourselves, ignoring the social rules of the time that young ladies should be chaperoned. It worked out well until one day while we were swimming in the pool, a group of teenage boys started to harass us. They laughed and tried to grab us. We finally managed to escape. While they hissed and jeered, we stormed out of there. We never went back.

It was the only time in Cuba I ever experienced that kind of threat, not on any bus, street, or in any other part of Cuba, chaperoned or not. When I told Johnny about this years later, he said this, and I quote: "Yes, we never cracked the MYC social exclusion. Others we knew belonged, but they seldom seemed to be there, such as Alice Sophie and Modesto in the later years. I think Olga was also MYC, but she later told me that she had rebelled against the meat market and refused to go. For some, maybe we weren't Cuban enough. Or maybe not 'old Cuban money' enough, and the same went for others like us."

I spent the rest of my summer reading *Gone with the Wind*. Curled up on the couch with Spotty, I was so absorbed in the book that the house could have collapsed around me, and I wouldn't have noticed. I was Scarlett O'Hara watching Atlanta burn and longing for Rhett Butler. I also wrote a lot of poetry. I was surprised one day when Mom confronted me about one of my poems. After sitting me down for a "talk," she pushed the poem at me. "What is this?" she asked.

"What?" I asked.

"You've never lied to me before. Now tell me about this."

I picked up the poem and read,

> She was an outdoor lass
> And a tough-bred lass was she
> With her hair of gold and her cheek of tan
> They called her the Lass of the Sea

> For many a moment and many a day
> Did she study the sea in bliss
> At the wide, wide blue
> And the white-capped waves
> As they swirled the sands a kiss.
> Now into the life of this beautiful lass
> This lass with a cheek of tan
> There came a love
> That was not a love for her sea
> For this other love was a man.

I stopped at this point and looked up at her, feeling uncomfortable.

"Is that you? Is there a man?"

"No, Mom. It's just a poem." I blushed.

"Well, don't write things like this."

"Okay."

Rhett Butler would have to wait.

In April 1956, we moved to *Playa de Marianao* on *Avenida del Golfo*. Mom started teaching English to adults at the Instituto Cultural Cubano Norteamericano near Havana. It was only because of this that she became involved with President Batista. He had contacted the institute because he wanted to hire a teacher to come to the Presidential Palace to tutor his little boy in English. The institute recommended my mother.

She had been going to the palace for a while when the news hit us one afternoon. The palace was under attack.

It was Mom's afternoon to be there. Dad raced down to rescue her. He was stopped by a barricade of militia and sent away. He spent the rest of the afternoon pinned to the floor in a nearby restaurant as gunfire echoed around him. He called us from the bar phone. We could hear the gunfire. Mom had already called us. She too had reached the gates of the palace. When they stopped her, she persisted in asking if Senora Batista and the little boy were all right. The guard told her they were and that they were inside in a closet with a mattress propped against the door. Mom quit teaching after that. Batista sent a dozen roses to her as an apology.

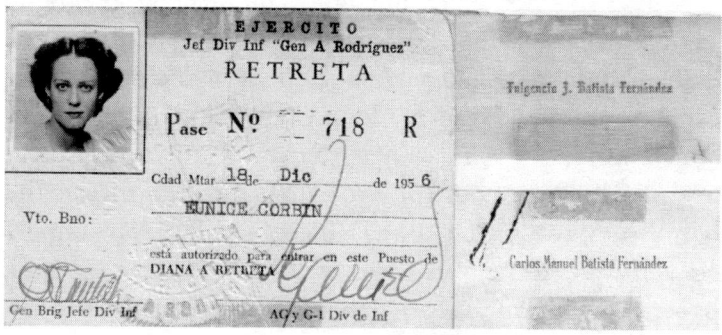

Mom's pass to enter the Presidential Palace.

Dad quit his job in Havana and was involved in building and owning a steak house called Delmonico. It was the first open barbeque grill in Cuba. It was just a few blocks from our house in the suburb of Playa de Marianao.

Hurricane Warning

Those last months spent in Cuba were among the most unforgettable I've ever witnessed. Johnny had graduated from Ruston Academy High School and had gotten a scholarship to the University of Chicago. He was home for Christmas break.

It wasn't a very good Christmas for anyone that year. It was the year 1958, just a few days before Castro took over. Everyone was scared to go out. Terrorists were setting off bombs in public places. Police were killing and being killed.

There was a strange, uncomfortable feeling at school. "The Americans support Dictator Batista," some of the Cuban students would say. "The shells of the bombs that explode around us read 'made in USA,'" others would add. And I would answer, "When your own army put Batista in there, how many of you protested, and who throws the bombs? Why do you always blame us for everything?" "If you want to help us, help us distribute some of these papers," one of my Cuban classmates said. She handed me a pile of pro-Castro leaflets. A black car with a man and a woman followed me home the next day and stopped me. The woman called to me in Spanish. "Come here, little girl." When I did not, she asked for directions to get somewhere. I gave them to her and kept on walking. Soon after this, my mother received a phone call. "'Tell your family that people who don't mind their business get hurt," the voice said, and then they hung up.

Delmonico, our restaurant, was a big steak house with about seventeen employees. Dad was having trouble with them. They had always been our friends and were as brothers to me. When I would bring one of my dates over for dinner, they would always tell me if he was okay or if I should steer clear of this joe.

Our bartender, Martin, especially was a family favorite. He was popular not only with the adult patrons but with all our school friends who came there, both Cuban and American. Whenever there was a teenage party anywhere, they would often end up at our restaurant, playing the piano and eating ice cream or drinking rum and Coke. Martin would stand behind the bar, polishing glasses and occasionally reaching up and smoothing his carefully placed elaborate hairdo with the one wave across the front.

He was always trying to learn English. He would approach one of the boys with "Hey, buddy. Comma—he, how you say," and he'd pull out his pad and pencil.

Then one day, Martin approached my father with the warning "Tenga cuidado, Senor. Tenga mucho cuidado." Everything does not go well, be careful what you do.

For months the restaurant had been losing money. People were not going out. There was no money to pay bills or wages. Now Dad wanted to close down and wait until better times to reopen. But it was not an easy thing to do.

According to law, nobody could be fired, and the employees did not believe him when he said he had no more money. All *Americanos* had money. Martin was referring to this. "They will do anything to fight you, senor. In times like this, we have no friends."

On my birthday, December 27, Martin disappeared. The cook had made a birthday cake especially for me and had allowed me to rummage in the ice creams and syrups. It was late, and Martin should have been there. He was to make me a Brandy Alexander. Martin's father showed up instead. Pale and shaking, he explained that two men in uniform, shouting and cursing, had come the night before and had taken Martin away after much questioning concerning some hidden arms. It was an old story. Young men disappeared, never to be found again. Sometimes their bodies would show up in the Almendares River, tortured and mutilated.

Through his Masonic connections, my father tried to find out where Martin was, but before he could do so, time ran out for Batista's sadistic police. Martin survived and was one of those released from the crowded Principe Prison the day after Batista fled.

On New Year's Eve, things picked up a little. The restaurant was more than half-full. We had decorated the dining room and hired a singer for the evening. A man seated with his wife and another couple threw his empty glass on the tile floor. Nobody paid much attention. A few minuets later, he threw another glass on the floor. Rene came in with a broom and started sweeping up the broken glass. People hushed a bit and glanced at the man. He had thrown his own glass and his wife's. Now they were arguing. He reached over to his friend's glass and raised his arm. Everyone had stopped talking and were watching him. He opened his fingers and let the glass drop. His friend was laughing nervously. His wife was embarrassed and was trying to make him stop. "I will not be polite in the restaurant of a Yankee," he said. Then he stood up, bowed from the waist to his audience, and ceremoniously dropped the other woman's glass. My father whispered something to Rene, who disappeared and came back with a tray full of empty glasses. My father took the tray and placed them in front of the glass thrower. He then took two slow steps back, bowed ceremoniously from the waist, smiled, and gestured with a sweeping arm over the floor for the man to continue. Things relaxed a little, and people chuckled. The man looked at my father dubiously. Another guest rose from his table and slapped the man on the back. "Relax, amigo. I know the owner. I come here often. He is a good and decent man and treats everyone well." The man grunted and ordered another drink, pushing the tray of glasses away.

EYE OF THE HURRICANE

We got home at five thirty that morning. At a quarter to six, the phone rang. It was Sol, my brother's Cuban girlfriend. "You're kidding," he said. "Halleluiah! Batista's fled the country!" he told us. By this time we could hear phones ringing all over the neighborhood. Lights were coming on in the houses. People were shouting. The radio was dead. The streetlights were dead. Excitement of the exhilarating sort heaved back and forth across the darkness. I felt like jumping up and down.

After a while, an excited, high-pitched voice came on the radio, confirming Batista's flight. He announced his program as Radio Rebelde. He said Fidel had come down from the Sierra Maestra Mountains and was on his march to Havana City. Everyone was to stay indoors until he arrived, and it was safe. All the men with authority had fled the city, and it was temporarily without government organization or police force. Everyone was to do their duty and behave. "The eyes of the world were upon us." *The old Cuba had ended. The new Cuba had not yet begun.*

The following week was spent as though we were living in a bomb shelter. Not even a stray dog could be seen on the streets. Every once in a long while, a car would speed by with self-appointed militia men crouched down in the seats, their rifles sticking out of the windows. Red-and-black kerchiefs were streaming from the radio antenna so as no one would mistake them as being on the wrong side. Sol and her dad volunteered for Red Cross.

Sol and her dad.

On the ninth of January, Fidel Castro reached Havana. My friend Esther Tato and I went down to the Malecon seafront drive in the city to see him go by. We waited for hours. The whole city had turned out to see him. Nearly everyone was dressed in black and red. The people were flooded into the streets along the line of march so that a car could not get through. After a couple of hours, everyone sat down, the men spreading their handkerchiefs under their wives.

When they came, they came in dribbles. First a motor scooter, then a jeep, then a couple of more motor scooters, then a few scraggly bearded soldiers on foot, then a tank and some more jeeps, all of them plowing their way through the excited, pressing crowd. "Atras! Atras!" they yelled. "Get back! Get back!"

"He's coming! He's coming!" the mass yelled. People were pushing and shoving so that I had no choice but to move with them. I could feel the buckles on my shoes being torn off by trampling feet. Esther, who was short, was having trouble breathing. "Stick your elbows out," I told her. I found a *barbudo*, a bearded soldier, in front of me, and a rifle pressed across my chest.

"Get back! Make way for Fidel!"

People were pushing in back of me.

"I can't!" I wailed desperately. At that he picked me up and set me on what felt like a moving ledge. I felt myself sliding back onto something soft, and then people were laughing and reaching down to help me up. I was weak with laughter myself as I sat up and found myself in an open crowded convertible that the *barbudo* had set me in. It was inching its way through the crowd. I sat up on the back of the seat and shouted along with the other passengers, "Viva Castro! Viva Cuba libre!" We were waving at the truckloads of shy bearded farmer soldiers. The faces of the passing crowd were jubilant. Some were fanatical, others were crying, all were shouting and waving. Esther was bobbing alongside of the convertible, holding on to the side. I helped pull her in.

"Did you see Fidel go by in the tank? He went right by us," she asked.

"No, I missed him," I answered.

"We're following Fidel into Camp Colombia to hear him speak," the people of the convertible informed us.

It seemed as though everyone was going in that direction by car or by foot. Everywhere along the way, people were lined up as if waiting for a carnival parade.

Along the way we picked up a *barbudo*. He sat beside me and gave me a bullet for a souvenir. We also picked up a man in a gray linen suit. He hadn't shaved for about two days and looked as if he were trying to join the *barbudos*. "We have protected our women and children. The eyes of the world are upon us. We've bought justice and peace with a clean revolution," he said as he waved benevolently at the crowd. "If Batista had stayed just one more day, I would have joined Fidel in the mountains," he assured us, twining his arm in brotherhood around the *barbudo's* shoulders.

We had to abandon the car half a mile before we got to the gates of Camp Colombia. People and cars and trucks and jeeps were jammed up, trying to squeeze their way through the gate. Esther and I would have been separated if we had not had our arms linked tightly together. We found that the man in the gray linen suit was somehow attached to our arms, pulling us through the mob. "Have you seen him yet?" he asked. At my answer, he gripped our arms so that we were one body of three, and he said, "You must see him! He is coming! He is coming in that tank over there!"

And off we went through the mob that was also trying to get to Fidel. If the mob was bad before, it was ten times worse now. "Keep moving! Just keep moving!" our supporter shouted at us as he somehow propelled us and yet acted as a buffer against the happy milling mob. I found myself suddenly jogging alongside Fidel's tank, and for about five breathless seconds that I shall never forget, Fidel Castro looked down at my jubilant face and saw me, and the expression that crossed his face was as though he was thinking, *And what in the hell is this crazy* Americana *doing here?*

Castro's tank passed, and the crowd joined ranks behind him, following his lead to Camp Columbia. We ran alongside military troop carriers full of staring, shy-looking *barbudos*. We waved and cheered them on, reaching up to soldiers for souvenir bullets they would take from their *bandoleros* slung across their chests.

"Sally!" a female voice said from one of the trucks. I searched frantically and caught a glimpse of a girl my age. She was dressed in fatigues and had a rifle slung across her back. It was Jo. I knew Jo from the Mother's Club. I waved and ran along beside her as long as I could. While Jo was from Havana, most of the soldiers were from the country. There were other women dressed in fatigues, with white chrysanthemums tucked in black hair that stood out against milk glass skin. It made me think of Marta. Maybe one of them would call out to me "Salion! Sahlee-on!" she would say. "Good-bye, good-bye," I would finally get to say.

With quick insistent maneuvers, our protector not only got us through the gates of Camp Colombia, which was acting like a broken floodgate for a tidal wave, but he placed us at a point of advantage: right smack in front of the grand stand where Fidel and his strongmen sat. Between us and the grand stand and running a borderline all around it stood the bearded soldiers with their rifles held across their chests.

"Have you been with him a long time?" our friend in the gray linen suit asked one of the soldiers in front of us.

"Fourteen months," the bearded one answered.

Our protector nodded solemnly, stroking his chin. "For years I have wanted to join him. Just one more day, and I would have. Just one more day," he said.

The *barbudo* ignored him. He was looking at the red silk scarf on my neck. A twinkle came into his eyes, and he reached over and took the end of the scarf gently between two fingers. "Por favor, Americanita. Please, may I have this as a remembrance to take back home to my wife in Camaguey? Please." He cocked his head shyly to one side. I glanced at Esther. She laughed and shrugged her shoulders as if to say "How can you refuse?" So I untied the scarf and gave it to him, wishing him and his wife well.

Fidel had finished conferring with his friends and had decided it was time to speak. He rose. The crowd thundered. He raised his hands. The crowd roared. He said something that was drowned out. The crowd became hysterical. I looked behind me and, for the first time, became frightened. A sea of flesh was stretched over the square, over the pavement, surging over the sidewalk and out and up over the sloping marching grounds. Fidel took a step forward. His right-hand man, Camilo Cienfuegos, was at his side. Right behind him, a huge Cuban flag billowed. Somewhere on the stage, they kept releasing white doves that flapped around. Fidel and Camilo took a step forward. The crowd surged forth, slamming us against the rifles in front of us. The breath was wrenched from me. I felt my knees grow weak, and then the faithful arm of our protector was under my arm. The crowd strained. Fidel was shouting. Several in the mob began to shout. "Let him speak! Quiet!"

Fidel raised his arms over the crowd. "Friends! I am proud of you! Let me first congratulate you for the clean and orderly revolution you have successfully completed!"

The crowd cheered. Our friend shouted, "We would all have joined you if we could have, our liberator! All of us! Every able-bodied man! We would have rid the streets of the filth of Batista!"

Fidel raised his arms, and the crowd quieted. He spoke. "Now I know every one of you are well-organized, clean-conducted citizens! I am going to come down these stairs and walk through the crowd to that speaker's stand over there. I know I will have no trouble reaching it! We are all grown and reasonable people!" And with this he promptly descended the stairs.

The mob parted.

"Come, we are going to stand next to the speaker's stand," our protector announced after Fidel had reached it. We got as far as a few feet from the stand, and then even our friend could get us no closer. Fidel started to speak. The crowd quieted. Our friend interjected his approval at various points, shouting and waving his arms frantically. "We are with you! The eyes of the world are upon us—upon you! Upon *you*—our Fidel!"

Fidel Castro stood on an elevated wooden platform about five feet high. Our protector became restless as time wore on. He wanted to get closer to Fidel. He inched us through the listening crowd until we were once again confronted with the protecting border of soldiers. "My wife feels faint. Please, may we sit under there?" he asked a soldier, pointing under the platform. The soldier looked dubious. "Please, then, let the women through! We must take care of the women! This has been too much for them." With this the soldier let us through, and Esther and I found ourselves sitting exhaustedly on the damp dirt looking up through the cracks in the platform at Fidel towering over us, a tame dove perched on his shoulder and the Cuban flag curtaining above him against the evening sky.

Our protector had forgotten us, standing out there in the crowd fighting his private war. He now must surely be right under Fidel, demanding acknowledgment as the number one member of the audience.

We were tired. My shoes were black with soot, and my shoe buckles were gone. It was dark and safe, somehow like a protective cage that gave us freedom away from the mob. I rested my head on my knees. Fidel swept his arm over the audi-

These two-sided leaflets were being handed out to the crowd. I was lucky enough to get an autograph from Camilo (Castro's right-hand man), who later mysteriously disappeared. Jorge Mendoza from Radio Rebelde also signed it.

ence, knocking over a glass of water that was on the railing in front of him. It shattered noiselessly on the platform.

Underneath, we watched the water drip through the boards and form rivulets and streams in the dirt.

The new Cuba had begun.

After this, life tried to seem normal. Schools started again. Businesses opened. People were out and about. Everyone was still on an emotional high. There was also an underlying feeling of uncertainty. Johnny was reluctant to leave us and fly back to Chicago. Dad was adamant that he go—and go now.

February 27, 1959. Spotty was killed. I had stopped by the restaurant after school, and Nona told me. As I walked past the cash register and out the door, I could feel her eyes on me, questioning why I wasn't crying. My legs carried me down the sidewalk. I looked up at the clouds. *It would clear up tonight*, I thought. I looked down at my brown loafers. They needed polishing, like the dead leaves crunching under them. At the corner, the cars whizzed by—cold steel that struck and hurt.

As I approached our house, the big boxer from next door ambled up to me, wiggling his stubby tail the way Spotty wouldn't be when I walked in the house. I knelt down and put my arms around the big wiggling neck and rested my forehead on his big brown head. Everything inside me crumbled. Visions of my life with Spotty flashed before me—the beaches of Rio where we had found him as a puppy, the farm where I had chased cows, Spotty running along beside me and climbing trees, Spotty waiting patiently for me to come down. I could feel him in my arms trembling during fireworks and hurricanes or snuggled safely every night under the bed covers. I wanted to cry. There were so many things you couldn't hold on to.

"Hola," a voice said from over my head. I looked up at my six-year-old neighbor straddling a tree limb. I released the wiggling dog that was waiting patiently for his friend to come down.

"Hi," I said and walked into an empty house. Silence surrounded me. I went to the kitchen hoping to find some cookies, and then I changed my mind. I sat down at the piano to practice. The noise coming from the keys seemed discordant. I got up and peeked out the window. The neighborhood seemed silent too. Was God mad at me? I started to cry.

The Writing On the Wall

Dad was increasingly alarmed as he listened to Castro's speeches on the radio and TV. Arrests were being made of anyone who looked suspicious. This included anyone who had been in Batista's armed forces who had not left. One of these included Jorge, Johnny's godfather, who had become

Let's Look At Today

I saw a frightening thing on television yesterday afternoon. The Prime Minister of the Republic of Cuba, Fidel Castro (sic), in violent harangue (there is no other word), asked the people of this country to disregard the verdict of one of his very own revolutionary tribunals that acquitted a group of forty-five flyers of Batista's air force accused of genocide, murder and assassination.

He stated flatly that in Cuba, today, you are either for or against the revolution. I am not against the revolution; but I reserve the right that that same revolution has granted me to write as I think; and I think that the Prime Minister has made a very great mistake in losing sight of the basic argument that has arisen from the revision of the trial of the acquitted flyers, a revision whose outcome is a fait accompli against the aviators after Dr. Castro's televised talk. This unfavorable revision is termed justice by Dr. Castro.

FIDEL CASTRO had an opportunity of becoming great yesterday. If he had merely criticized the decision of the court that acquitted the flyers, and allowed it to stand, without insisting on a revision and demagogically and violently bringing enormous pressure on the decision of the revisory court against the accused, he would have shown himself to be a man who respected the tribunals of his own government and who adapted himself to their decision; but Dr. Castro, from the very beginning, has always had it in for the flyers, and the decision of the court has thrown him into a frantic rage that imposes his will upon the matter.

Reprisal, reprisal, reprisal is the theme that ran through Castro's words. He accused the defending lawyers of pettifogging, he accused them of using the trial, not to state their juridical position, but to further their political aims. In an unparalleled attack against the moneyed classes of the country, in an attack on money per se, he accused the defending lawyers of becoming tools of these interests and serving coun-

"Let's Look at Today" (two sided)

a pilot in Batista's air force. He felt he was just Cuban; this is where he belonged. Whatever Cuba wanted he was comfortable with. Castro saw him as an enemy. Jorge was to spend the rest of his life in prison.

March 8, 1959: Blindsided

"Go home and pack your clothes. Use just one suitcase, and put in only your good clothes. Don't tell anyone. Don't call anybody. No one is supposed to know. We are leaving in the morning." These were the instructions Mom gave me when

I walked into Delmonico. Castro had not yet stopped the ferryboat that sailed from Havana to Key West.

At home, I joined Nona and Granddaddy, who were throwing things into our station wagon. There was no time to think. I wished later that we had put in our Cuban oil paintings and my school yearbooks. Fortunately, we did include our scrapbooks and family photo albums. We piled the clothes that we couldn't take onto Winnie's bed. It was her day off, and she hadn't been told either. We couldn't take a chance and didn't want to implicate her.

Just before dawn, my grandparents opened up the restaurant. Their best friends, Miguel and Rebecca Jimenez, were to go and pick them up later in the day. They were to say there was an emergency and just walk out. Miguel

> ### Government By Hysteria
>
> Fidel Castro may go down in history as the only dictator who tried to stand a sugar quota against a wall and shoot it.
>
> Castro has taken another step down the dictator's pathway. He has denounced the United States as the prime cause of his ineptitude and the chief reason for Cuba's chaotic internal situation. His speech before the presidential palace was nothing more than Hitler's big lie spoken in Spanish.
>
> A brief review should be sufficient. The man of the mountains cannot recollect that the United States made a present of independence to Cuba at the end of the Spanish-American war. He cannot reconcile the economic fact that this country gives Cuba a preferred position in the sale of its chief commodity, sugar. He rejects the avid American support he received as a revolutionary who was to usher in an era of "democracy" by destroying the dictator, Batista.
>
> Cuba is in trouble because Fidel Castro is following a Red-oriented, if not Communist-directed, program of organized chaos. Government in Cuba is by decree of Castro, not by consent of the governed. Mob rule is the order of the day.
>
> Economically, Cuba is near bankruptcy. The right to hold private property has been lost in Castro's program of "agrarian reform." Business functions on a day-to-day basis. Utility rates are fixed by decree at levels which will insure a loss. The all-important sugar industry simply may not exist in another year if the sugar-producing lands are broken up by decree. Tourism which once brought a flood of welcome American dollars has been seriously curtailed.
>
> Level-headed Cubans who were happy to see Batista driven into exile have finally spoken out against this Red decay. Others living in the United States have taken part in the protest.
>
> But now that he finds governing is vastly different from rebelling, Fidel Castro attacks the only country which offered him overt aid. Castro was widely hailed as Cuba's man of the people by the liberal press.
>
> It may be mentioned that a strange and strained silence hangs over those American editorial voices which hailed Castro only a few months ago. Those who decry mob rule in Southern states somehow cannot transfer their indignation a short distance to oppose mass hysteria just across the Florida Straits.
>
> The situation grows more worrisome with each passing day as Castro tries to substitute oration for sane administration. This country can permit Castro to move just so far down the road to communism. But there is a point where self-interest begins to concern the United States, too. Without making a choice for them, this country can take steps to permit the Cuban people to choose a government which can face facts without resorting to hysteria.

"Government by Hysteria"

and Rebecca were to take them to the airport where they would then fly to Miami.

As Mom and Dad and I were driving away, we passed Winnie walking up from the bus stop. I stuck my hand out the window and waved. She lifted a hand toward us. This time, she did turn white. Somehow, she knew.

We got out just in time. Dad could see the writing on the wall. He had seen the signs before in South America. He knew Castro was a Communist. We were able to drive our packed-to-the gills station wagon right onto the ferryboat. We sailed out of Havana Harbor and past Morro Castle for the last time.

Several hours later, we drove off the boat at Key West. When we drove into Miami, we were relieved to see Nona and Granddaddy sitting on their luggage at the door of the airport. It had been a long day.

The ferry with Corbins on board.

PART 2

Hello, USA

THE AFTERMATH

Hello, USA

We moved in with my great-aunt Nana in Coral Gables, Florida. We were all happy to be together, although Johnny was still in Chicago. Danny, Nana's thirty-year-old parrot, recognized me instantly. I had taken care of him when we lived on the farm. Ruffling his feathers, he instantly flew to my shoulder and announced, "Danny is a pretty boy."

Danny is a pretty boy.

I was excited. Florida felt familiar to me. Maybe I was home again. Here I could speak English everywhere.

Yet one day, I found myself on the bus going to the store, listening to the Spanish of a jabbering group of Latin-looking young men. A pretty young student was standing next to me in the aisle, books pressed against her hip and smiling sweetly, oblivious to the fact that the men were discussing her anatomy in a bluntly sexual manner. They were obviously feeling protected and at liberty to do so because of the language barrier. As the discourse peaked, I exploded and blurted out in Spanish for them to shut up and that what they were talking about was "muy feo" (very ugly). Amid stunned silence and very amused stares that seemed to say "Did you really just say that, and where in the hell did you come from?", I got off the bus.

Mom had enrolled me right away in Coral Gables High School. The school was so big that on the first day of class, I got lost in the hallway. I was always late for every class. In something called homeroom, I was finally assigned a "big sister." Becky took me under her wing. She became my anchor. Without her I would have been adrift. It was more than halfway through the school year. Everyone already had their tight social circle. Fraternity pins were pinned on to sorority sweaters, and each hallway was the meeting place for a different "club." Football heroes were the idols of the school. Prom queens reigned. To this scene add me—long wavy dark blond hair and Spanish-style hoop earrings in pierced ears. "Not the style here," Becky warned. It wasn't *in*. I kept my earrings *on*. I was familiar with not being *in*.

Back at my aunt Nana's, the heat was overwhelming. In Cuba, at least there was always a breeze. I sat on the back steps feeling alone. My parents had moved to Indiana where Dad found a job promoting a new advertising agency. I was praying for just a whisper of freshness against my clammy skin. I raised my left hand toward the sky, pleading for a storm, or hurricane if necessary, or anything familiar that might sooth my discomfort and bring me a sense of belonging. As I looked up at my hand, I decided to draw it.

Fifty years later, that drawing would find its home on the pages of this story. But for a long time, life would whirl on around me. Cuba was ninety miles to the south, and I was neither here nor there, still caught in the deceptive eye of the hurricane, in the middle of nowhere. Home would be a long while coming.

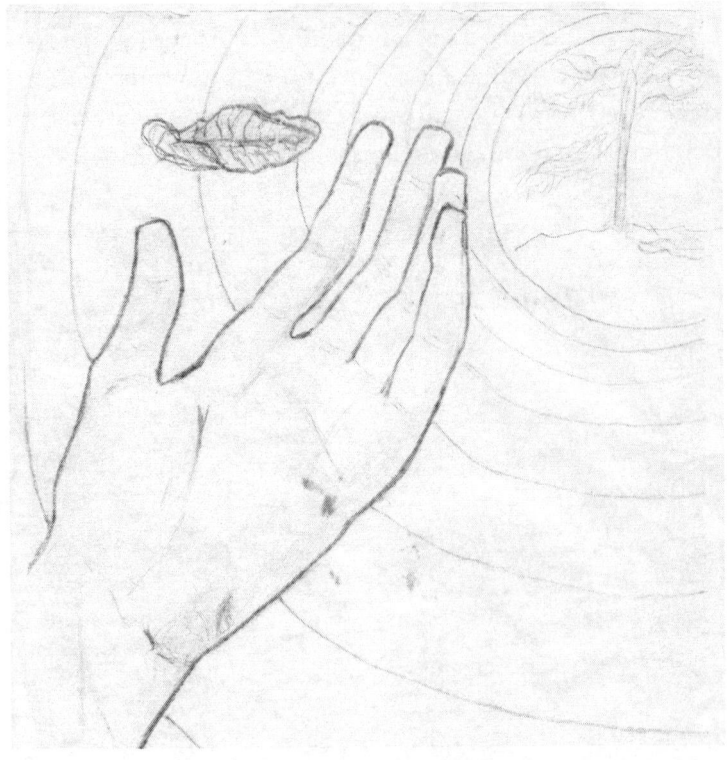

Drawing by Sally Corbin, 1960.

WHISTLES AND GUNSHOTS

Marriage, two kids, the Beatles, and the Kennedy clan would shape the early part of my adult life. Most of our friends were lost to us. Some we would find again. During the Bay of Pigs invasion, we would be informed by Mr. Gilbert, a fellow American from Cuba, that a mutual friend, Mr. Anderson, who had owned Shell Gas in Cuba, had been captured. He was accused of delivering arms to the underground and was captured and imprisoned in Morro Castle. When the Americans didn't continue the assault, Mr. Anderson was put in front of the firing squad and shot. Mr. Gilbert remembered that when his friend got angry, he always whistled. He bet that Mr. Anderson was whistling when they blindfolded and shot him.

My first child, Carl, was born soon after John Kennedy's assassination. My second child, Rick, was born just before Bobby's assassination. We were on vacation in Mexico when it happened. We heard the news of Bobby's death on the taxicab radio. When the cabdriver dropped us off at the airport, we had all bonded so much that he gave us all a hug.

My grandfather died in 1962. My mom died in 1965. Nona died in 1969. Johnny lived in Spain and now lives in England. He was a professor of anthropology at Kent University in England until he retired. Dad died in 1995. In the ensuing years, I would live in four different states and twelve homes.

Dad, Johnny's wife Marie, Johnny, me, Carl, and Ricky. Family reunion late '70s.

RECONNECTING

Sally and Terry, Christmas 2011

Christmas 2011: Wisconsin

Once again, Terry and I are sitting by the fireplace. The cardinals and blue jays are dining at the feeders that Terry hung in the snow-covered pine trees. It's been three years since I took the journey back in time. Much has been remembered and written about, some of it already written in my youth. I make the commitment now to finish capturing the journey on paper. The memories of deadlines of the Cathedral School newspaper when I was assistant editor impose themselves in my head. Cutting and pasting become a passion again. Connecting with some of my childhood friends along with the "remember when" stories helps bring my days in Cuba back to life.

Rocky Harper was a great help in these reconnections. Earlier this past year, he suddenly appeared in my living room. He was on TV in a documentary on the History Channel about Castro's Cuba. It introduced him as an attorney from Miami. The first thing next morning, I tracked him down on e-mail. Rocky got me in touch with more of my other classmates. This story is about all of us, heard from or not. We all lived this. We were all together at that point and place in time, and that one event that blew us all asunder from here to there and then finally back to wherever we all are now. We landed on our feet. We su vived. I raise my glass to toast us all. "Salud!" And as Tiny Tim said in *A Christmas Carol*, "God Bless us, everyone."

How did I get to Cuba in the first place? People are always asking me that. My answers were always vaguely illuminating. But my big brother Johnny is here to shed the light, which follows in part 3, "How Did We Get There?"

Still landing on my feet.

PART 3

How Did We Get There?

By John Corbin

THE ANGLO-HISPANIC FRONTIER

The Havana that my sister and I grew up in was, in fact, on a frontier between Anglo and Hispanic America, a frontier that had been in existence for more than three hundred years and, for most of that time, had been moving south. Fifty years earlier, our great-grandparents and grandparents had been among those Americans who had pushed it farther south than it had ever been before, but in 1959, it was now about to return north, taking nearly all Americans living in Cuba and nearly a million Cubans with it.

Not that we thought of Havana as a frontier. For one thing, *frontera* meant the border separating one state from another, and our home was in Cuba, not on the border between Cuba and the United States. For another, *frontier* implied wild country with few people, and our home was in a bustling city. But in past American experience, the frontier was beyond the borders of the state, usually sparsely occupied by tribal Indians but sometimes claimed by another state, such as France or Spain. In either case, it was where Americans met people of another culture speaking another language. It is in this sense of a meeting place of peoples of different cultures rather than a political border separating two states that I want to use *frontier*.

The Spanish arrived first, establishing themselves in the Caribbean in the early 1500s with their administrative capital in Cuba, the largest Caribbean island, from which they launched their exploration and conquest of mainland north, central, and South America. By 1521, they were exploring the land they called La Florida, establishing permanent settlements as of 1565. The resulting Spanish colony of Florida nominally covered most of what is now the southeastern United States from the Atlantic Coast to the Mississippi River. It had very few Spaniards, mostly soldiers and officials in settlements that were little more than fortified villages and priests in widely scattered missions.

The possibility of an Anglo-Hispanic frontier arose when in 1607, England established the colony of Virginia to the north of La Florida, but there were so few people living in such widely separated settlements that contact was very limited. As the English were more interested than the Spanish in occupying land and farming it, their population grew more quickly. Political boundaries were moved south with the founding of first the province of Carolina in 1663 and then the colony of Georgia in 1733.

The few Spaniards living in these areas were displaced to a reduced Spanish Florida with borders much like those of the present state, though extending much farther west along the Gulf Coast. In 1763, the border shifted south again when Spain ceded Florida to Britain in exchange for Havana, which the British had invaded and occupied. The ethnic frontier between Anglo and Hispanic America also moved for most of the Spanish in Florida simply left when it became British.

The British had little time to populate Florida before the American Revolution began in 1776. The small Anglo population had yet to develop any distinct sense of identity as Floridians, and the colony did not seek independence from Britain. In the treaty that established the United States of America after the war ended, the movement of border and frontier south was reversed for the first time for in 1783, Britain gave Florida back to Spain.

This reversal lasted less than forty years. Once again, Spain did little to occupy and settle Florida or defend its borders. American settlers drifted across, and as the newly established United States regarded Florida as a lawless haven for runaway slaves and renegade Indians, there were armed incursions, including a US military expedition. By 1820, Spain was beset by political instability at home and wars of independence throughout Hispanic America. In 1821, Spain ceded Florida to the United States on condition that the United States stop its people from entering the Spanish colony of Texas. Just as in 1763 when Spain wanted the city of Havana more than the whole of Florida, in 1821 they wanted Texas more than Florida.

American settlers continued moving south, gradually coming to grips with mosquito-infested swampland better suited to the native alligators, poisonous snakes, and scorpions.

In many ways, this "taming of the South" was like the much more famous taming of the west, complete with Indian wars, big cattle ranches, and railroads. Florida offered a peculiar attraction of its own; warm winter weather and much railway expansion was driven by that attraction. The railways would build a big resort hotel in some attractive location at the same time as they built the railway to bring guests from the north to the hotel. Often there were no or few other people or facilities in the place, so the railways were keen to encourage people to settle there who could provide the guests and staff of the hotel with medical, legal, and commercial services.

In midcentury, Florida entered the Union as a slave state. Cuba had not joined the rest of Hispanic America in revolution, but not all Cubans were content with Spanish rule, and some wanted Cuba to follow Florida and join the United States as a slave state. This annexation movement received some support from the southern American states who wanted help in the looming conflict with the antislavery north. Had the movement succeeded, the US borders would have moved south, a stage further to include Cuba. Americans would have flooded into the new state, and the resulting Anglo-Hispanic frontier in Cuba would have been inside the borders of the United States. Instead, the movement ended with the defeat of the south in the American Civil War of 1861–1865 and the abolition of slavery in the United States, and Cuban opposition to Spanish rule took another tack. In 1867, a major political crisis in Spain gave Cuban nationalist leaders an opportunity to declare independence. By doing so, they set off thirty years of intermittent and mostly guerilla war for Cuban independence. In 1898, the United States declared war on Spain and sent a small expeditionary force to join the Cubans in their War of Independence. Spain was defeated, not so much in land battles in Cuba, but more in sea battles where the American fleet proved far more effective than the Spanish.

In Cuba, Spain capitulated to the small American army, much to the annoyance of Cuban officers who felt that they had been winning the land war in Cuba before the Americans arrived. The American command immediately ordered that Cuban troops be confined to their bases and disarm. They then proceeded to set up an occupation government. Americans flooded into the island. Many hoped that Cuba would become American, but the occupation government established a constitution modeled on the United States and, after a couple of years, gave power to the Cubans and withdrew.

Not, however, without qualification, for Cuba was forced to accept the terms of the Platt Amendment, which significantly limited Cuban sovereignty. Cuba was required to give the United States land for military bases but prohibited from doing so to any other power; it was required to govern the country as the United States would have governed it, balancing the budget and maintaining public sanitation; it was required to grant the United States the right to intervene should Cuba fail to keep those terms but prohibited from allowing any other country to do so. The most curious provision concerned the Isle of Pines, the eighth largest island in the Caribbean off the southeast coast of Cuba. Though long administered as part of the colony of Cuba, it was to be "omitted from the proposed constitutional boundaries of Cuba, the title thereto being left to future adjustment by treaty." Though stopping short of promising that the Isle of Pines would become American territory, it left open the possibility that if Americans did as their forefathers had done—occupying frontier land, establishing farms and communities, founding churches and schools, governing and policing themselves correctly—they could apply for inclusion in the state. In less than a decade, the Isle of Pines was remarkably Americanized.

Understandably, many Cubans resented the Platt Amendment, even if in 1906, one faction of Cubans in conflict with another invited the United States to intervene, which it did, occupying Cuba again until 1909.

Increasing opposition from Cuba was matched by increasing reluctance of the US government to supervise. By 1925, the United States had renounced all interest in taking over the Isle of Pines, and in 1934, the governments of Cuba and the United States agreed to revoke the terms of the Platt Amendment.

Despite the failure to make Cuba into US territory, the American presence continued to grow. Soon, Cuba was replete with American residents and imported American institutions—English-language churches, clubs, schools, newspapers, radio stations, boarding houses, and hotels—which coexisted with the native institutions of the much larger Cuban population. American sports such as baseball and boxing were introduced and quickly adopted, and even Cubans who could not speak English could discuss last night's fifth inning *honron por el lef fil fens* or third round *nocaot*.

Unresolved tensions made the country politically unstable. The revolutionary movement that triumphed in 1959 confiscated land, businesses, and other property and established a socialist economy.

Most of the Cubans who left went to Miami and there proceeded to do what Americans had done to Havana in the first half of the twentieth century. Despite the best efforts of annexationists and colonizers, the political borders between the United States and Cuba had not changed since 1821, when the United States acquired Florida, but the Anglo-Hispanic frontier that had been in Cuba between 1898 and 1959 was now in the United States, firmly ensconced in south Florida.

AMERICANS IN CUBA

Typical of Americans in Cuba in the first decades of the twentieth C were my kin, thirteen of whom moved to Cuba between 1905 and 1920 and the men that three of my great-aunts met and married there. The oldest were three of my great-grandmothers. One of these, Moleska Gates, accompanied her second husband, and they brought with them their two young daughters and an older daughter from Moleska's first marriage, my grandmother Eunice Miller. My step-great-grandfather Gates was an archetypical temporary expat, a businessman from Ohio posted in 1910 or thereabouts by the American company that employed him to work in its newly opened Cuban subsidiary. After a half dozen or so years, his tour of duty ended, and he returned to Ohio with Moleska and their two daughters, none of whom ever lived in Cuba again. Not, however, with his stepdaughter, for she had married and chose to stay in Cuba with her husband.

The other two great-grandmothers, Corrie Fowler and Mary Corbin, were widows brought to Cuba by their sons.

Their husbands, Samuel Mills Fowler and John H. Corbin, both had grandparents who were originally from the coastal area north of New York City but moved west to central upstate New York to settle farms in the early 1800s. There, both their fathers were born and grew up then moved farther west in midcentury, in the Corbin case to Friendship in the southwestern corner of New York, in the Fowler case much farther to Michigan. So both families were part of the general movement of Americans westward at the time.

The Corbins then settled down for a generation. John H. was born in Friendship, married Mary there, and never lived anywhere but the southwestern corner of NY state. Even during the Civil War he stayed put. Four of his brothers joined New York regiments and saw action outside the state, but he was a bit too young.

In contrast, the Fowlers remained mobile and far ranging. When the Civil War began in 1861, Samuel Mills was nineteen, and he joined a Michigan cavalry unit as a bugler and served throughout the war, finally being mustered out in Texas in 1866. He then studied homeopathic medicine in Cleveland and Chicago. After qualifying in 1870, he married Corrie, also qualified in homeopathic medicine, and moved to practice in Des Moines, Iowa, where his children were born. In 1883 the generations-long Fowler migration west became a migration south with a move to Deland, recently founded in central Florida. Some years later, the family moved again to Saint Augustine where Samuel

Mills became physician to Henry Flagler, the railway magnate. At that time the railway that connected Florida to the north stopped in central Florida. Julia Tuttle, a widow from Ohio who had moved to south Florida in 1891, wanted to develop the land she had bought on the Miami River and to that end had petitioned Flagler to extend the railway. He was not convinced until the severe winter of 1894–1895 wiped out the citrus crop in north and central Florida, and Julia Tuttle took or sent him orange tree branches to show that the Miami River area had not been affected. Tuttle offered Flagler free land to build the railway station and a hotel. In 1896 the railway arrived, the building of the hotel began, and the three hundred or so adult male residents voted to incorporate as Miami. The population began to grow, and the Fowlers were part of that early growth for Flagler helped move them there and become established in the new resort town. In 1898 when Julia Tuttle fell ill and died, Samuel Mills and Corrie Fowler were her doctors, and in the same year their daughter Corrie married Julia Tuttle's son Harry.

By the end of the century, the mobile Fowlers had reached south Florida, but the Corbins were still living in upstate New York. That would soon change. John H. and Mary's son, my grandfather, Samuel, was an electrician who went to Saint Louis in 1903 to prepare the site for the Louisiana Purchase Exposition, otherwise know as the St. Louis World Fair of 1904. Perhaps it was there that he learned about the opportunities for Americans to colonize the Isle of Pines for in 1905, he was living on the island and, shortly after, brought his widowed mother and his two teenage sisters, Eva and Bess, to live with him, first to run a boarding house for Americans and later a family farm. The plan seemed to have been for the women to maintain a family home on the island year round where he would join them for the winter months, returning north to work as an electrician in the summer. Both sisters married American men in the Isle of Pines, Eva in 1910 and Bess in 1911, but Samuel married Myrtle Miles in Chicago in 1911, and it was in Chicago that his three children, John E. (who was my father), Eleanor, and Richard, were born. The marriage broke up, and in 1920 so did the family, for Samuel took the two eldest children, John E. aged seven and Eleanor aged four, to live in the Isle of Pines, leaving the infant Richard with his mother in Chicago.

Although the Corbins had leapfrogged the Fowlers to reach Cuba first, the Fowlers soon followed. During the second US military occupation of Cuba (1906–1909), the army hired Samuel Mill's and Corrie's son, my other grandfather Frank, as a civilian surveyor and sent him with a crew to draw up a map of the land and buildings, including the Moro Castle, around the bay of Havana. When the job ended, he stayed on in Cuba and brought his mother (his father had died in 1899) and younger sister Faye from Miami to live with him. The women eventually returned to Miami, but not until Faye had met and married a young American, much as the Corbin sisters had done in the Isle of Pines at about the same time. Frank too met a young American in Cuba, Eunice Miller, and married her. Their only child, my mother Eunice, was born in Cuba.

Frank was employed for a while by the Henry Clay Bock Tobacco Company, Cuban founded, named after an American presidential candidate and at that time British owned. Athlete, boxer, and weight lifter, he was one of the Americans who brought boxing to Cuba, refereeing professional matches, establishing a gym, and training and managing prizefighters (among his charges was the young Eligio Sardinas, who later under the name of Kid Chocolate became the first Cuban to be internationally ranked, winning the world junior lightweight crown in 1931 and the featherweight championship a year later).

Like his step-father-in-law, Frank was an expat, living outside (*ex*) the fatherland (*patria*). In contrast, the Corbins who left the United States for the Isle of Pines thought they were taking the land of their fathers with them. When it became clear that the Isle of Pines would continue to be Cuban, most of the Americans living there repatriated. So it was with the Corbins. Mary and Bess and her husband went to live in Tampa. Samuel moved his children to a farm near Mango, which was not far from Tampa. If the Fowlers reached Cuba by way of Florida, the Corbins reached Florida by way of Cuba. The exception was Eva, who moved with her husband to run a boarding house in Havana. By the mid-1920s, most of my American-born kin had returned to the United States. The Gates were long gone, as were Corrie Fowler and her daughter Faye. Frank and Eunice Fowler still lived in Havana with their daughter, but of the Corbins only Eva chose to stay on as an expat.

The two youngest of those who had left would return, but at different times. In 1927, Samuel Corbin died, and Eva came from Havana to collect the twelve-year-old Eleanor whom she and her husband adopted and raised in Cuba. Bess assumed responsibility for the fourteen-year-old John E., enrolling him as a boarder in Montverde School near Orlando in central Florida. On graduating he went on to the University of Florida but had to drop out after a year for it was the height of the Great Depression and times were hard. He then became an expat again, going to join his sister and aunt in Havana. There John E., my father, met and married Eunice Fowler, my mother. There my sister Sally Ann and I were born. There too my aunt Eleanor married a Cuban doctor, Armando "Cuco" Loret de Mola, and their son Armand was born.

The 1940s saw another family exodus from Cuba. In 1944 my father was hired by Sterling Drug and was posted first to Brazil and then to Colombia, where we lived the lives of typical American temporary expats, keeping company mostly with other Americans. My Fowler grandparents, who had been living with us in Havana, decided to move to Miami. For them this was their first repatriation. My aunt Eleanor experienced her second, moving with Cuco to Illinois where he became the expat, qualifying to practice in the United States and become a small-town doctor. They were to visit Cuba frequently until the revolution but never live their again.

At this point my great-aunt Eva was the only one of us still in Cuba, but in 1949, my father quit his job with Sterling and returned to Havana, where we were soon rejoined by my grandparents. By this time Eva was a widow, and after a few years she decided to move to Miami where her sister Bess was now living with most of her children and grandchildren. In 1959 when the revolution triumphed, my grandparents, my parents, my sister, and I were all that were left, and we too would soon be gone. Over the years, thirteen of my American-born kin had come to settle in Cuba. Five of these had married there, a further four, including me, had been born there, but none of us still live there and none would die there.

AMERICANS OF CUBA

Of the many Americans who came to live in Cuba, only some stayed on. Because they did, some Americans *in* Cuba became Americans *of* Cuba. There were five such among my kin: my sister, mother, grandmother Eunice, aunt Eleanor, and I. Three of the five had been born in Cuba but two had not, so it is not necessary to be born in a place to be of that place. These two, my grandmother and aunt, were young enough when they came to Cuba to learn to speak Spanish with a Cuban accent, important because to be of a place when you sound foreign in the language of that place is hard. More important was growing up in Cuba, and most important of all was growing up with Cubans, not just with Americans, for it was perfectly possible for Americans growing up in Cuba to have very little to do with Cubans. The five who were Americans of Cuba all had close Cuban friends as they grew up, and the three who were Cuban born had Cuban godparents, extending these friendships over generations. Working relations with Cubans also extended over the generations. Gonzalo, my grandfather's assistant when he had his gym and handled boxers, became a kind of family retainer, called upon by my father whenever help was needed with jobs like moving house, replastering rooms, or selling strawberries on Sundays from a roadside stand, this last with me as his twelve-year-old assistant.

All this meant that families could be very mixed. My Corbin grandparents, Samuel and Myrtle, were both Americans, but she, as stable as he was mobile, lived in Chicago her whole life, while he unintentionally and temporarily became an American in Cuba. Their three children were born in Chicago over a period of just five years, but Richard, like his mother, remained an American in America; my father, like his father, became an American in Cuba for a while; while Eleanor, the only one to grow up in Cuba, became an American of Cuba. The three were reunited in middle life when John returned to Chicago and Eleanor lived in rural Illinois, but in later life the force of where each had grown up took over. Richard, as far as I know, stayed on in Chicago. My father retired to Orlando, just a few miles from Montverde where he went to school. Eleanor couldn't return to Havana, but she and Cuco did the next best thing, moving to Miami when he retired.

Samuel's sister, Eva, who moved from being an unintentional American in Cuba like her brother to an intentional and long-term one, established an even more mixed family. She and her husband were Americans in Cuba, but her adopted daughter was an American of Cuba. Eva, widowed after Eleanor left home and not wanting to live alone on the small farm near Havana she had moved to when she and her husband sold their boarding house, fostered Lolita, a child from a nearby village. Living with Eva as she grew up, Lolita learned to speak English without a Cuban accent and was educated as an American. She was a Cuban who, while still in Cuba, became in effect a Cuban of America. As a young businesswoman she moved to Chicago then married a farmer she met at Eleanor's home and has lived in the United States ever since.

These family mixes affected how I grew up. The first time I went to a nightclub, drank alcohol in public, and got home at six o'clock in the morning, I did so with a family group made up of a Cuban in America (Cuco), a Cuban of America (Lolita), three Americans of Cuba (my mother, Eleanor, and myself) and an American in Cuba (my father). In December of 1954, Eleanor, Cuco, and Lolita were back in Cuba for the holidays. Cuco was in a festive mood and managed to get a table for New Year's Eve at the San Souci nightclub on the outskirts Havana, and he asked my parents to join them. Even though I was only fourteen, I was asked too, mostly because Lolita had no partner, loved to dance, and I could dance to Cuban music. When we settled at the table, Cuco ordered Coca-Colas and a bottle of Bacardi. My aunt began pouring rum for cuba libres, and when she got to the glass in front of me, she gave me the same amount of rum she had given the adults. Until the small hours of the morning, I watched the Cuban floor shows, drank cuba libres, and danced to Cuban music.

Americans of Cuba experienced particular ambiguities and ambivalences, especially the Cuban born, who legally were both Cuban by birth and American by descent. In appearance, my mother could have been Cuban—she had the right shape, height, and, except for green eyes, coloring—but my sister and I were too tall, thin, and fair. Cubans who didn't know us usually assumed that we were American, though any who learned that we were Cuban born might question that assumption. But even those who knew us well were aware of the limitation of appearance. My closest Cuban friend once introduced me to another Cuban as "the oddest Cuban you have ever seen in your life" ("El Cubano mas raro que ha visto usted en su vida").

Americans also assumed we were American, sometimes with an insistence that made me uncomfortable. For example, one day my father and I were driving along the seafront when we were stopped by a group of agitated boys who had been swimming. A boy had half-drowned, and they wanted us to take him to the nearest first aid station. We did, but when we got back, we found that the boys were still there, the crowd now swelled by passersby. The boys thought that one was missing, might still be in the water, and were uncertain about what to do. I was thirteen or fourteen years old at the time, a strong swimmer, and had had lifesaving training at scout camp a year or two before. I asked my father whether I should go in. He said yes, and as I was stripping down to my underpants, I heard one of the boys in the crowd say "Wait, wait. The American is going to go in" ("Espera, espera. El Americano se va tirar"). I found the boy floating underwater about twenty yards out. By the time I got him back to the shore, the police had arrived. They took the boy from me, put him in the squad car, and raced off. Unfortunately, he had been underwater for more than half an hour and was dead.

The next day the *Havana Post* reported the incident, following it up with an editorial praising me for courage and my father and me for being Americans selflessly helping Cubans.

This praise was at odds with what I had felt. There was absolutely no physical danger to me in what I had done; the only "courage" I showed was that required to strip to my underpants in public. At no time did I think of myself or my father as Americans and the boy and the crowd as Cubans. The only identities at play beneath the surface in my mind were those of scout with lifesaving training (itself a nice mixture as the scout organization to which I belonged was the Cuban national one, but the scout camp where I had learned lifesaving was American) and child in relation to adults (my father, without whose agreement I would not have gone in, and the police, who, by taking the boy from me, had stopped me giving him artificial respira-

EDITORIALS 6/9/54

THE CRUEL SEA

Without in any way wishing or endeavoring to see out of focus a set of circumstances which could present themselves at any time in any community, THE HAVANA POST is proud to commend publicly the action of a father-and-son team, John Edward Corbin, and John Edward Corbin, Jr., in helping to save the life of a young Cuban boy, Nestor Pestana Marrero, on Sunday last.

As has already been related in this newspaper, the Corbins were driving out towards Miramar when an excited crowd asked them to take a boy, 11-year-old Nestor Pestana Marrero, to the nearest first aid station. They complied immediately and while the father was driving the car, young Corbin applied artificial respiration and was successful in restoring the process of breathing in the victim before they arrived at the station.

Upon their return to the "Las Playitas" beach, the Corbins found that there was considerable discussion as to whether or not another boy was missing. Finally it developed, after a check of the clothes on the beach, that a pair of shoes was without claimant. Young Corbin immediately plunged into the waves and finally located the body of another boy, Ricardo Ruiz, 11, about three feet below the surface. He brought the body to the beach, but unfortunately it was too late for human aid to be of any service. Ricardo Ruiz was dead.

One is justified in wondering what went on in the mind of John Corbin, Sr., while his young son was swimming around under the surface of the cruel sea which had just menaced the life of one young Cuban and perhaps had already claimed another Cuban boy as its victim. But it was the cause of humanity and neither father nor son faltered.

All of us regret that young Corbin was minutes too late. But the courage he displayed and the spirit which sent him into those treacherous waters in the hope of being able to save the life of another human being cannot be too highly commended.

Neither of the Corbins seek any publicity for their actions on Sunday last, but we feel that the fine example that they set may well be cited in these times when the spirit of exaggerated nationalism is abroad in many parts and the country to which they belong, the United States of America, sometimes is impugned by persons of ill will. Young Corbin did not stop to ascertain the nationality, race or religious creed of the missing boy. Another human being was in danger, and John Corbin, Jr., was ready to expose his own life to endeavor to save that of the boy who was missing.

John Corbin, Sr., is associated with Publicidad Inter-Americana, S.A., and because of that connection is well and favorably known to THE HAVANA POST. But he also is a former employee of this newspaper, and we are all the more gratified in those special circumstances to be able to say to both father and son, "Well done. Very well done, indeed."

Dear friends,

On behalf of the Members of the British Club and the entire Anglo-American Colony I desire congratulations to the Corbin family for the fine demonstration of manhood and brotherly love for the preservation of life related herein.

John Watson
6/10/54

tion). In any case, there were other identities involved. I was white, and the boys were various shades of brown; I had learned swimming and lifesaving, and the boys were from poor families that gave them no such opportunity. Havana had no natural beaches, but the well off could join the private clubs with their man-made beaches, saltwater swimming pools, and yacht basins. The nearest public beaches were hours away by public transport that the poor could ill afford. Looking back, it seems to me that the real story here was the lack of opportunity and a safe place to swim for the poor, multihued children of Havana, a story to which nationality was incidental.

I again felt uncomfortable some years later when my high school principal pressed me to enter a DAR contest for the best speech on the duties of the American citizen in Cuba. Reluctantly, I agreed, thinking that I might get away with the mild subversion of arguing that the duty of American citizens in Cuba was to behave like Cubans. There must have been some mild subversion among the judges as well because I actually won the contest.

Not that Cubans expected Americans to be able to act like Cubans. The practice at Ruston was to have an English-language play for the students in the American high school and a Spanish-language play for the students in the Cuban *bachillerato*. In my junior year in high school, I had already appeared in several English plays. A friend in *bachillerato* told me she was going to try out for the Spanish play, which that year would be directed by her mother, a professional in the Cuban theater. She urged me to join her, and I decided I would, even though no American that we knew of had ever had a part in the school Spanish play. To my surprise, I got one of the main roles. That the director had been a close friend of my aunt Eleanor when they were growing up and that when I went out with the director's daughter I did so Cuban style (with chaperone) may have had something to do with it. Casting an American in the Spanish play seemed to have raised some eyebrows for when the play was over, I learned that the formidable head of *bachillerato* had said that she had come "to laugh at the American" ("reirme del Americano") but in the end approved my performance.

Experiences like these with family, family friends and retainers, and my own friends and teachers, with Cubans and Americans, helped form the adult I was growing up to be. My sister lived in the same places at the same times, shared the same home, had the same family, knew the same people, belonged to the same clubs, and attended the same schools. She and I had become Americans of Cuba like our mother, aunt, and grandmother before us. So had some of our contemporaries, but we were the last Americans to do so. Half a century on, there aren't many of us left.

—John Corbin, AB with special honors in anthropology, University of Chicago, PhD; social anthropology, University of Kent at Canterbury.

REFERENCES AND ACKNOWLEDGMENTS

The analytic distinction between the Anglo-Hispanic ethnic frontier on the one hand and the political border between English and Spanish colonies and their successor republics on the other is my own, but I would be not in the least surprised to learn that others had used it or something similar. The same is true of the distinction between Americans of Cuba and Americans in Cuba.

The Rev. Harvey M. Lawson's exhaustively titled compilation of the *History and Genealogy of the Descendants of Clement Corbin of Muddy River (Brookline) Mass. and Woodstock, Conn: With Notices of Other Lines of Corbins*, published by Hartford Press in 1905, has a brief reference to my grandfather Samuel as well as longer entries for all of his Corbin forbearers. Mark Voorheis, the town historian of Friendship, New York, where my great-grandfather John H. was born, showed me documents that, among other things, supported part of a Corbin family story—that two of John H.'s brothers had served in the Union Army during the Civil War, been captured, held in Andersonville prison, and survived (but not, of course, the whole story) and that they were the only brothers to get out of Andersonville alive. Thanks are due to Susan Snyder, a former resident of Friendship who was researching the Corbins, for sending me copies of documents about Samuel and for resolving an anomaly in the Friendship cemetery records. Thanks too to Bette Stockman of Friendship for putting me in touch with Susan Snyder.

Tom and Melissa Fowler maintain a Fowler webpage that contains an article summarizing their knowledge of six generations of Fowlers. Brief biographies of the two Samuel Mills Fowlers, my great- and great-great grandfathers, are included. The staff at the town library of Deland in Florida pointed me to material that led me to correct two Fowler family stories: that my grandfather Frank was the first baby boy to be born in Deland (he was a child when the family moved there) and that Julia Tuttle was his sister (she was in fact the mother-in-law of his sister).

Jane McManus offers a lively and readable account of the American presence on the Isle of Pines in *Cuba's Island of Dreams: Voices from the Isle of Pines and Youth,* published in 2000 by the University Press of Florida. Boris Goldenberg's *The Cuban Revolution and Latin America* was published in 1965 by Allen and Unwin in London and Praeger in New

York. Boris was living in London when I went there as a graduate student in 1962, just before the original German version of this book was published. He told me that he doubted that Fidel Castro had been a Communist before he took power. His brother Raul had indeed long been a Communist, but Fidel himself was simply an ultranationalist. Nor had Fidel presided over a socialist revolution, for inasmuch as the process was a revolution, it was not socialist, and inasmuch as it was socialist, it was not a revolution.

Much academic analysis has focused on the impact of American culture on Cubans, perhaps the most comprehensive of which in English is Louis A. Perez Jr.'s *On Becoming Cuban: Identity, Nationality and Culture*, published in 1999 by the University of North Carolina Press. I have found no corresponding academic analysis of the impact of Cuban culture on Americans in Cuba. My own "*Cubanos*, Americans, and Modes of Being Between in Pre-Castro Cuba," which appeared in volume 26, number 3 of the *Third World Quarterly*, attempts a broader analysis of the interplay of Cuban and American cultures and identities in prerevolutionary Cuba.